VISUAL MEDIA FOR TEENS

◆ ◆ ◆

Creating and Using a Teen-Centered Film Collection

Jane Halsall and
R. William Edminster

Libraries Unlimited Professional Guides for Young
Adult Librarians Series
C. Allen Nichols and Mary Anne Nichols, Series Editors

LIBRARIES UNLIMITED
An Imprint of ABC-CLIO, LLC

A B C ⬯ C L I O

Santa Barbara, California • Denver, Colorado • Oxford, England

Library of Congress Cataloging-in-Publication Data

Halsall, Jane.
    Visual media for teens : creating and using a teen-centered film collection / Jane Halsall and R. William Edminster.
        p. cm. — (Libraries Unlimited professional guides for young adult librarians series)
    Includes bibliographical references and index.
    ISBN 978-1-59158-544-2 (alk. paper)
  1. Libraries and motion pictures.   2. Motion picture film collections.
3. Libraries—Special collections—Video recordings.   4. Libraries and teenagers.   5. Teen films—Catalogs.   I. Edminster, R. William.   II. Title.
    Z692.M9H35   2009
    016.791430835—dc22   2009020300

13 12 11 10 09   1 2 3 4 5

This book is also available on the World Wide Web as an eBook.
Visit www.abc-clio.com for details.

ABC-CLIO, LLC
130 Cremona Drive, P.O. Box 1911
Santa Barbara, California 93116-1911

This book is printed on acid-free paper (∞)
Manufactured in the United States of America

Dedicated to Sarah, Anne, and the teenagers
of McHenry Public Library District

CONTENTS

Contents

SERIES FOREWORD

We firmly believe that teens deserve equal access to library services, and that those services should be equal to those offered to other library customers. This series supports that belief. We are proud of our association with Libraries Unlimited, which continues to prove itself as the premier publisher of books to help library staff serve teens. This series has succeeded because our authors know the needs of those library employees who work with young adults. Without exception, they have written useful and practical handbooks for library staff. We're glad to have these two new collaborators add their names to that list.

Just like books, movies provide teens with entertainment and can introduce them to a variety of issues and characters. People from every generation have all found movies that define who they are and current teens are no different. Teens love this visual medium, and we as librarians should take note. This book helps you, as a teen librarian, connect more closely with your audience. You will find great ideas on programming, collections, and issues in dealing with movies in a library that will support your current services.

We hope you find this book, as well as our entire series, to be informative, providing you with valuable ideas as you serve teens, and that this work will further inspire you to do great things to make teens welcome in your library. If you have an idea for a title that could be added to our series, or would like to submit a book proposal, please email us at lu-books@lu.com. We'd love to hear from you.

Mary Anne Nichols
C. Allen Nichols

ACKNOWLEDGMENTS

This whole journey happened because people told us that we could do it, that we had something worthwhile to say, and the teens we were and the teens we know caused us to recognize the importance of this book.

The authors would like to thank our past director, Arlene Kaspik, who encouraged us for many years in our speaking and writing, as well as our current director, James Scholtz, who gave us his conviction that we could finish the book.

We wish to thank the Board of Trustees of the McHenry Public Library District for their unexpectedly strong support, as well as our families, friends and the staff of the McHenry Public Library for their patience, understanding, and support.

Sarah Halsall del Rio deserves special thanks for reading the manuscript and making suggestions.

We want to thank the teen patrons of the McHenry Public Library for allowing us to become part of their cultural and pop cultural lives and trusting us enough to talk to us.

We especially want to thank the teen who, when asked what his favorite movie was, answered *Duck Soup*, because he validated our decision not to underestimate the willingness of teens to try and appreciate new things.

INTRODUCTION: THE TEENAGE YEARS ARE AN AWKWARD AGE...FOR LIBRARIANS

While libraries generally boast excellent track records in serving both young children and adults, teenage patrons often find themselves neglected. As common as this is, it obviously should be avoided, for when we let teenagers fall through the divide between our service to children and our service to adults, we lose them as patrons, particularly male teens, until they are adults with children of their own. Fortunately, the situation has begun to change as new librarians graduate and enter the work force, motivated to serve teens by their own experiences both with libraries that gave them what they were looking for when they were teens and libraries that did not.

One effective technique for drawing in teen patrons, then keeping them, is to create a teen feature film collection that is both exciting and tailored for teens. Movies can be a big draw for teen patrons. This works especially well when you listen to your young adult patrons and then tailor your collection to the teen population of your community. Our teen patrons suggested to us many of the films discussed in this book, and their suggestions helped us bring teens into our library. We believe these suggestions can serve as a starting point for the reader's library.

Our intent in writing this book is to help librarians serve teens by sharing what has worked for us in building a strong teen collection. We assume that librarians who consult this book perceive a need in their library for either a new collection or for a shake-up in their current collection. We don't recommend simply buying everything we list and leaving the situation at that. Each community is different, so these selections can only be a starting point to spark interest and inspire recommendations from your teens.

You will find few resources on feature films for teen library collections. At the time of writing, we found no film selection guides for librarians serving teens, and no existing periodicals with reviews of feature films specifically intended for library selectors of teen materials. Of course, there are fan Web sites that can be useful, but they are by and for fans, and as such often fail to mention details that are critical for selectors. This book provides a guide for selectors who serve teens by informing them of films that are current, popular, and available, and by providing guidance on how to identify relevant films that teens will find enjoyable.

Teen collections are usually the responsibility of either the children's or the adults' departments. As a result, service to teens in the past was a secondary responsibility within a department, receiving less attention and resources. Dealing with teens often became a predicament or burden rather than a joy for staff whose primary objective was to work with children or adults. That's why we say that the teenage years are an awkward age for librarians.

Teens are not children; nor are they adults. They tend not to give positive feedback as easily as children, and as a general rule they are less articulate and forthcoming about what they need than adults. However, teens can be delightful and rewarding patrons if you get past the awkwardness that may come from a teen's uncertainty about how to interact with librarians in particular and adults in general. The positive change in attitude among younger librarians towards teenage patrons coincides with an increase in the number of librarians who specialize in serving teens. This is commendable and is definitely a change worth welcoming; however, new librarians are often more comfortable helping teens that have needs similar to the ones they themselves had when they were young. For example, a person who became a librarian because he or she loves books may not recognize the needs of a patron who loves films, videogames, and music more than reading. What this ultimately means is that although there are now more librarians to listen and respond to teen patrons, the increase in staff does not necessarily mean better service to all teens. It often still leaves teens who are not bookish without an advocate. Hiring a young adult librarian with the enthusiasm of a missionary does not guarantee that the teens being served will end up getting what they really need.

A teen collection of any type, whether books, films, or other media, must be built with respect for teens, and must never be assembled by default or by relying exclusively on the librarian's personal tastes. The key to a successful collection is to engage young adult patrons as often as possible, and once their confidence has been gained, to ask them directly what kind of selections they would like to see. Also, be sensitive to their opinions, open to their experiences, and willing to respond without judgment. Be aware of generational differences. Be ready to accept that what was great when you were a teenager might be a dud now. However, look for films that aren't obviously aimed at teens but contain the elements of appeal that we list below. Look especially for films that contain teen characters that your teens can identify with; the presence of a teenaged character is not enough. If you try a film and it doesn't work, remove it.

Once you have asked your teens what they want, listen to what they say, and act on it. If you treat teens with interest and respect, they will respond and realize that you take them seriously. Teens will check out what you have, suggest more titles, and even tell their friends that the library is a pretty cool place.

The films listed in this book are primarily intended for popular material collections. While many if not most of the recommendations are entertaining, they also deal with moral, social, and personal issues, and are therefore appropriate for school library collections. These films are examples of currently available and older pivotal films, both cult and mainstream, that allow teens to see characters that resemble themselves on the screen.

Our list is not comprehensive and we are sure you will be able to come up with a number of valid suggestions for a teen collection. You must remember that even your most obvious suggestions will not work in every collection and must be tested.

AUDIENCE

This book is primarily intended for librarians who wish to build a teen feature film collection or who see that their current film collection does not serve their teen patrons' entertainment and informational needs. The book provides a broad list of films with teen appeal and offers advice on selecting new films for your collection as they become available.

We developed this book from a series of presentations that culminated in a presentation at the 2004 Public Library Association Conference in Boston. As we considered why certain films worked in a teen collection, we found that it wasn't useful to talk about traditional genres and borrowed the concept of "appeal" from readers' advisory terminology. The categories we've identified helped us to predict choices that proved to be popular with teens in our library.

Film collections tend to be browsing collections, so appeal needs to be built in during the selection process. Identifying items that will appeal to your teens will lead to a collection with high circulation.

If you are required by your library's selection policies to only select films that receive good reviews, you may be dismayed to see that we list films that we're critical of in some way, even describing some films as mediocre. Teens haven't honed their critical skills when viewing films and can enjoy a film that a more sophisticated viewer would find appalling. For that matter, many very popular films have justifiably received bad critical reviews. Feel free to disregard any films we describe as mediocre, but don't be surprised if your teens ask for or recommend them for purchase.

While a film may be flawed from a critic's point of view, it can also be inspiring, uplifting, and exactly what a teen needs at that moment to grow on. At one time, librarians felt that their collections should include only high-minded, worthwhile books, but we now realize that libraries need to include popular materials as well. We want the public using the library and getting their tax money's worth. Some readers and viewers will develop the critical judgment to move from the mediocre to the classics, but that's not our concern as long as they get pleasure from and use our collections.

MOVIE RATINGS AND TEEN FILM COLLECTIONS

Defining the target age for a library's teen collection is a local decision based on community conditions and standards. Unless it is clearly stated somewhere in your collection development policies, the decision may be left within the purview of each individual selector. A teen collection aimed at junior high school students only necessitates a different approach to selection than one aimed at high school students and early college age teens.

We have included some films that could not have been selected for our library's teen film collection based on the films' R ratings. These films appeal to teens who are 18 or 19, and can be recommended through Viewers Advisory where appropriate. It's possible that the teens you are advising have already seen these films on cable, watched them with their parents, or had them checked out for them by their parents.

We have included films with a wide range of ratings to provide suggestions for purchase, as well as to make librarians aware of the type of films that might be requested. If you are aware of these titles, you might be able to suggest "view-alike" titles that are in the library collection, and that are perhaps even more appropriate. Viewers Advisory has existed informally as long as libraries have had popular feature film collections, which in many cases is not very long, but it has not had the professional attention paid to it that Readers' Advisory has. This may reflect librarians' attitudes toward films and popular culture as opposed to books, which librarians tend to take more seriously.

Perhaps you bear the responsibility for purchasing film for all collections within your library, and, if a title is not appropriate for the teen collection, you can purchase it for the adult collection. We have worked with the adult film selectors at our library, using money from the teen film collection budget to purchase films appropriate for older teens, but that will ultimately be shelved in the adult collection.

Movie ratings appear to be a blunt instrument, without subtlety. As a librarian, you need more information to make precise decisions about whether a film belongs in your teen collection. A film may receive an R rating based on language that a teen wouldn't even notice as being vulgar. A film rated PG-13 may also contain violence that makes it much too troubling for your teens.

Sometimes a rating has to be interpreted. One site worth consulting for teen film selectors is Common Sense Media, www.commonsensemedia. org, a site that provides reviews that address controversial ratings and may help the selector decide whether a film conforms to the library's definition of a teen film collection. We discuss the Common Sense Media Web site more fully in the chapter "Film Reviews and Resources."

You can find out what a rating means and whether it makes a film inappropriate for your teens by watching the film yourself. You will begin to notice that ratings vary by the decade they were given. Older films sometimes have their ratings changed from R to PG-13. Films can be released in a PG-13 and also an unrated version that has more explicit language, violence, or sexual imagery. Watching helps you understand why a film was rated the way it was and whether you can still recommend it to some of your teens.

Be aware of your library's policies on challenges to materials. When a patron challenges a title, listen sympathetically without being defensive. Visual depictions of an event, whether in films, graphic novels, or picture books, can be more upsetting than a description. If the problem arises because someone who is younger than the target audience is using your collection, this is a wonderful chance to do Viewers Advisory and steer the patron to the correct collection. If the patron feels that an item needs to be removed or moved to the adult collection, follow local procedures, and start pulling together your reasons for keeping the item.

The nature of visual media like films or graphic novels, and even picture books, means that a few images can seem more important than their context. A film may be challenged based on only one or two scenes that are intrinsic to the film and not gratuitous displays of sex, language, or violence. The films in a teen collection are not intended for children, and sometimes parents, and, more dangerously, selectors may try to make the teen collection as safe as a children's collection.

You are selecting for your local community and community standards will vary. Community standards need to be learned, sometimes by testing them in controlled situations like teen review boards or by asking teens you have a relationship with to view and report back. We can become so concerned as selectors not to upset our patrons that we limit our collection unnecessarily and become the censors we're afraid of.

Whenever possible, we have watched the films we've listed. About a quarter of the films have been included based on trusted suggestions by teens, professional colleagues, and through reviews without being viewed by the authors. The teen suggestions came through formal and informal interviews, as well as surveys done in the library. You will find that if you make your teens comfortable talking about films with you, they will inundate you with their suggestions. Teens, especially male teens, will rave about their favorites. Colleagues are a good source of suggestions, although their suggestions may need to be tested by talking to actual teens.

Once you come to see how successful the categories of appeal we outline are, you will feel confident testing your own hunches about forthcoming titles. Quirky titles are especially fun to see become popular, and it's neat to be able to tell colleagues that you predicted the next word-of-mouth classic for teens.

This book is not intended to be comprehensive, but the compulsion among teens and colleagues to suggest titles has expanded not only the breadth of the titles included but also the depth in time covered. We've included *Midsummer Night's Dream* (1935) and *Rebel Without A Cause* (1955) as well as films that were in the theater and had not been released on DVD when we were writing this book. All the films listed were available or forthcoming in DVD.

ORGANIZATION OF CHAPTERS

In the first chapter, "Creating a Teen Film Collection," we talk about some general issues regarding creating a collection, such as what sorts of films appeal to teens and belong in a library collection, how teens learn about films themselves, how to deal with potential resistance for having a teen collection, and technology and format issues you may face.

Chapter 2 is "Getting Teens Involved," in which we expand on a primary theme of our book: talk to your teens, listen to your teens, and act on their suggestions. We give advice on putting on successful programs to get teens into the library and that make teens comfortable about letting you know what they want to view.

Chapter 3 is "Films Exploring Issues of Identity: Suggested Films." In this chapter we discuss the appeal of and list films that explore identity through coming of age stories, belonging or not belonging to groups, and the differences between cultures and nations.

Chapter 4 is "The Appeal of Heroes: Suggested Films." Teens enjoy and benefit from the stories of heroes overcoming adversity since they are themselves living the hero story as they face the world. Heroes come in many forms.

Chapter 5 is "The Appeal of Strong Emotions: Suggested Films." The appeal of fear and of laughter is especially strong for teens, as the film industry has learned to its profit.

Chapter 6 is "Education and the Arts: Suggested Films." In this chapter we explore feature films that offer opportunities for both entertainment and education. Who would have expected that films based on Shakespeare's plays and documentaries would be popular teen fare? We also explore musicals, filmed performances, and books that have been made into movies.

Chapter 7 "Film Reviews and Resources" provides information on where to find film resources in print and online.

Our afterword sums up the points we consider most important.

Remember that a static collection does not appeal to teens. The lists in this book are meant to serve as a beginning point only. Including these films in your collection is the first step. Ruthlessly weed titles that don't work. Use titles that circulate well as a basis for buying similar titles. Consider the recommendations in this book as a way to entice teens into the library, so that you can start a dialogue with them and find out what films they want to see in their library.

1

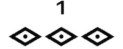

CREATING A TEEN FILM COLLECTION

For the purposes of a creating a teen film collection, it's best to discard the idea that teen films are a genre, although certain titles, such as *The Breakfast Club*, *Sixteen Candles*, and *Pretty in Pink*, inevitably come up when the topic arises. John Hughes created these and other very popular and very successful films in the 1980s that recognized the uniqueness and individuality of teens. These films raised the bar for all films aimed at a teen audience. Previously, films marketed to teens followed insultingly simple formulas, were set in unreal worlds without moral dilemmas, and treated teen characters as one-dimensional with limited room for growth. Fortunately for everyone, teen characters since the success of John Hughes's films have demonstrated growth and experienced realistic challenges as well as defeats. Even teen comedies that rely on gross-out humor and sexual innuendo now offer their teen characters an opportunity to grow.

We have based our organization of films on broad categories of appeal that represent what teens look for and enjoy in movies rather than on traditional genres, although some genres fall comfortably into one or another category of appeal. When selecting films for teens, look beyond the genres, and consider how the films would fill the needs of living, breathing teens.

The films that most truly deserve the name teen films are those in which the characters deal with transitions that mirror those in the lives of real teenagers. "Coming of age" is a term that can be applied to this kind of film, but movies in which characters of different age groups face loss of innocence, development of wisdom, and growth of self-confidence leading to maturity, also deserve to be included in a teen collection as honorary coming of age films. The common thread among these films is a discovery of one's identity that can happen on many levels—as an individual, as a member of a clique or outcast group, as a member of an ethnic or cultural group, or as a sexual being.

The appeal for teens of films that explore identity is that teens are going through this process themselves. First of all, an exploration of identity makes for an interesting story that teens can empathize with and simply enjoy. The films model teen behavior and reassure teenagers that they can get through similar situations themselves. Humorous films reassure teens by showing them the worst that can happen and demonstrating that their lives aren't as bad as they could be.

Although they might not seem an obvious choice at first glance, many superhero films mirror a teen's life experience in addition to appealing through wish fulfillment. Heroes with extraordinary powers try to deal with their profound differences from others, their innate special abilities, and the thrill of being able to do things they could only fantasize about before.

A film collection for teens needs to contain more than just films that mirror a young adult's experience in becoming an adult. Humor and horror films are especially attractive and important for a teen collection. Teens find a great appeal in strong emotions safely delivered via the movies. In order to have a popular collection, you need to include some video junk food, and there are many wonderful examples of humor and horror that you will be happy to have your teens discover.

Music performances are obvious additions, but the popularity of documentaries among teens may come as a surprise. Documentaries have become popular for all ages in recent years, as filmmakers have learned to entertain while informing the viewer.

TEENS AND POPULAR CULTURE

It's fascinating to discover what a well-educated and intelligent teen doesn't know about the world. A large part of being a teen is learning what older people know and can't remember not being aware of. Teens experience the joy of discovery but are also burdened with the stigma of being naïve even when they're well informed.

However, if you start with the premise that teens are completely naive and unaware of the larger world, you are displaying ignorance about the huge body of common knowledge shared among teens. Teenagers may not talk about business, the economy, or a lot of other adult topics, but adults do talk about favorite films, sports, and popular culture topics. However, conversation among teenagers is more likely to be about their popular culture passions, especially new things they've just discovered. Teens are also more likely to try new films, music, or books based on their friends' suggestions. Teens are less likely to prejudge music, films, and writers, and are more eager for new experiences than adults. Thanks to recent technological advances, a teenager's circle of friends might include Internet buddies who live on the other side of the world just as easily as it does the neighbor next-door. The upshot of this global networking is that information about fads and trends can spread between teenagers much more quickly and on a much wider scale than in previous times. Teens can be connected to each other, communicating in real time, even when separated by multiple time zones or great distances, and even as their parents worry that their teens spend too much time alone in their rooms.

Teens swim in a cultural soup unfamiliar to the typical adult. As interminable as the teenage years are for parents and teens, they are relatively short and pass rapidly. People enter and leave their teenage years and the networks associated with teenage culture at a rapid pace, while that culture evolves rapidly as well. A person who is in his or her 20s and setting up an adult life starts to drop out of contact with the shared teen culture. Older adults are more distanced from teen life since in addition to being out of touch with the face-to-face networking of teens, they are not likely to be involved in the social networking groups that 20-year-olds might still be connected to.

Teens are very receptive to pop culture influences, particularly those introduced to them by other teens. As a librarian, you can take advantage of this by attending closely to the interests and needs of teen patrons, then by making sure that appropriate items are available in the library as they become heavily sought after. There are few greater joys in a librarian's job than being able to put an item immediately into the hands of a teenager when he or she requests it. Having new hot titles on the shelves also helps your teen collection gain credibility and provides browsing teens the opportunity to find items of interest on their own, without having to ask an adult for recommendations—often the kiss of death for the recommended titles.

A teen's choices in popular culture, especially with regards to music, may result in his or her being identified (or identifying) with a particular social clique. These choices and their corresponding social labels have a tendency to be much more fluid for teens than they are for adults. Generally speaking, the average adult's tastes in popular culture tend to ossify and become associated with a narrow period of time, so that it is possible to estimate an average person's age by his or her music and pop culture tastes. Unlike adults, who tend to have a fixed canon of music, films, and books, teens are typically in an exploratory stage; they are still investigating what it means to be fans of anime films, for example, or fans of punk music. Teens listen to their friends to decide what's exciting or satisfying, and their tastes in music, films, and books is still being created. Since the technology available to teens means that their circle of friends can be much wider than in the past, the popular culture suggestions they receive can be much broader. Teenage tastes can be varied and eclectic even though they are often influenced by other teens.

Adults tend to jump to quick conclusions about their likes and dislikes based on their experience. For example, adults may determine that they don't like foreign films based on one or two unfortunate experiences, or they may decide that the only music they like is heavy metal. This is a common method of constructing patterns of likes and dislikes, and it undoubtedly simplifies life, but it nevertheless reduces one's openness to new things that might be interesting. Teens, however, are still determining their interests and discovering new things, so they aren't likely to know where the boundaries between genres are set. Because so much is new to teens, recommendations from trusted sources can be valid for them. They are at a stage when Homer Simpson and Homer's *Odyssey* bear equal cultural weight. If, as a librarian, you can become one of your teen patron's trusted sources, you can open a dialogue with the teen that will benefit the library's collection as well as the young adults who utilize it.

The difference between the current generation of teens and earlier generations is that there are so many more resources available today, and those resources are often accessible all of the time. One of the authors spent an evening with her young adult daughters watching the 1992 David Lynch film *Fire Walk With Me*, the prequel to the 1990s cult television series *Twin Peaks*. During the movie, the young women discussed each scene while consulting the Internet, looking for sites where the movie had already been thoroughly dissected and analyzed by a huge online fan base. Consider how difficult it would have been when the film was released to access a worldwide fan base and find critical information about a film that not only bombed, but was based on a television show that was cancelled after only two seasons. Now, however, this kind of instantaneous exposure and access to information is a fundamental reality of teen life.

The Internet delivers the world to a teenager, and it can also serve as a channel through which a teenager's creativity reaches the world. It is in this fashion that teens end up both the consumers and producers of electronic popular culture—for example, a teen can create films on his or her own camera and then distribute them to the world via computer.

Films today influence, and are influenced by, music, games, books, and television. This synergy feeds on itself and as a result the boundaries between types of popular media break down—for example, the lines between a film and a computer game end up blurring as the quality of video game graphics approaches that of big budget films. Essentially, electronic games are movies that anyone can star in, and may in fact represent what films of the future might look and feel like.

The Internet allows large groups of teens to interact in Massively Multiplayer Online Role Playing Games (MMORPG) such as World of Warcraft. These games become farther-reaching each day and frequently extend beyond the gaming world as people form close friendships with other players. Social networking due to MMORPGs is a growing phenomenon, as is the technique of *machinima*, short for machine cinema, the phenomenon of personal movies as developed by electronic gamers. These movies are often based on gamers' favorite games, and are typically rendered using the engines from those games. This production technique is discussed in more detail later in the book.

Music has a significant place in every teen film whether it is for developing character, advancing the plot, or building emotion. Music is also used to promote films, sell soundtracks, and generate music videos based on films. Apple's development of iTunes has revolutionized the music industry and offers almost any available piece of music for instant download. Selectors of teen films and selectors of teen music need to work together, since demand for a film will often lead to demand for the corresponding soundtrack.

THE LIBRARIAN'S ROLE

Ask your teen patrons about their personal interests as a way to learn how to improve and expand your teen collection. Though they might be reticent at first, most teens will open up and share their interests with someone who expresses and demonstrates sincere interest in them. Listen to what your teen patrons have to say and consider how to satisfy their needs through the library collection.

Even though a film has been recommended by a teen, it might actually belong in the Junior or Adult Collections at your library. Although we don't think you are required to watch every film you add to your collection, the more you know about the films you add, the better your collection and service will be.

As soon as you have a feel for what will appeal to your teen patrons, develop a routine for staying on top of the wide choice of online sources of reviews and film information aimed at non-librarians. Library review sources that serve librarians so well for other library materials don't cover feature films in terms of selection, much less in terms of selection for a teen collection.

Find a reliable Web site for new film releases, such as Reel.com (http://www.reel.com), which lists new DVDs each Tuesday. Set up a regular time to check whichever Web sites you use and look for likely choices for the teen collection. You can find annotations aimed at fans or businesses, and Reel.com links to reviews when available. Fan Web sites offer reviews, but you need to read them with a critical eye.

Check both film and DVD releases on fan and industry Web sites. Patron demand for DVDs starts while films are in the theaters so it's necessary to be aware of films you might be asked about. Check DVD releases to make sure you order the DVDs and have them available as soon as they're released.

Look for films that are released directly to DVD. This used to indicate that the film was not up to standards, but increasing numbers of direct-to-DVD films appeal to niche tastes that may appeal to your teen patrons. Movies created for cable television go directly to DVD as well.

Check print and online catalogs from jobbers and publishers such as those from Ingram, Baker & Taylor, and BWI. There are no film distributors that specialize in teen films for libraries, so check the companies your library uses for purchasing films for children and adults. The majority of purveyors of books to libraries have moved into providing films and music as well.

We recommend going to video and electronics stores, and, while browsing for bargains, striking up conversations with other shoppers, especially teens, and asking for recommendations. Every teen we've run into is eager to share his or her favorite titles with someone who's interested.

You may not be a teen but you're likely a fan of movies. Think about your favorite films and consider whether they fit our guidelines for teen appeal. (Don't take it personally if your choices don't circulate.)

A teen collection is primarily a browsing collection and gives librarians an opportunity to promote cultural literacy without pressure. Include a sprinkling of film classics that are part of popular culture in your teen collection, but do it with a light hand. An excess of older films will make your teen collection seem like a required reading list. Add films that are entertaining and that have widely quoted dialogue. Teens may recognize the titles and pick them up out of curiosity.

Some suggestions are films by the Marx Brothers or Woody Allen, *Casablanca*, *Gone with the Wind*, or perhaps *The Godfather*, if your policy on ratings allows it. These titles weren't made to be classics; they were made to entertain and to make money. However, the quality filmmaking craft that went into them resulted in films that are integral to popular culture and great works of art.

You can also entertain and enlighten teen viewers by providing the works that current films quote or rely on as their predecessors. Fritz Lang's classic silent film *Metropolis* is a good choice when you also carry Hayao Miyazaki's critically acclaimed anime of the same name. Some anime series are based on great English literature—for instance, the futuristic anime series *Hakugei: Legend of the Moby Dick* might tempt a teen to watch the classic 1954 black-and-white film *Moby Dick*.

Be sure to follow through after you've put these suggestions into your collection and pay attention to the circulation figures. If a classic doesn't seem to be drawing interest from teens, try featuring it in a display. If it still doesn't circulate, overcome your sentimentality and consider it for weeding.

Something to consider when evaluating your teen collection is that many adults, especially those under 30 years of age, often continue to read, watch, or listen to products of teen culture and as such might browse your teen collection. Your collection may have high circulation when it isn't actually serving teen patrons; teens need a collection aimed at their tastes. Remember that a perfect collection for teens is constantly changing and evolving. When your teen collection is part of a popular materials collection, and only adults are interested in checking an item out, it needs to go—either into the adult collection or out the door.

If you listen to your teens and act on their recommendations, your collection will become a trusted source of entertainment. Take as your goal the experience of early iPod users who were considered cool by definition.

Early users of the iPod would stop each other on the street and plug into each other's iPod to listen to the music the other person had been listening to. Similarly, if you carry the films, music, and books that teenagers recommend, teens will take that as sign that the titles they don't recognize on your shelves are worth watching, listening to, or reading.

ARGUING FOR A TEEN FEATURE FILM COLLECTION

It is sometimes necessary for libraries to prove to taxpayers or administrators the value of a collection or a service. While you may find the need for a teen feature film collection to be self evident, it might not make sense to everyone at your library. Budget constraints limit the choices that librarians can make. Some libraries simply don't have the money or the space to create a collection aimed at teen patrons. However, public librarians who are limited by space or financial constraints can still make use of this book to ensure that their teen patrons have access to films that serve their needs, without having to build a distinct collection.

Some libraries do not collect feature films, using the rationale that those films are likely to be available through commercial outlets. Policies such as this reduce the demands on a library's budget, as well as the potential for conflict with local businesses. Some libraries may instead choose to collect nonfiction films, such as documentaries, how-to guides, and biographies, since commercial outlets are less likely to carry them and because these films generally serve the educational needs of the community. You'll find some nonfiction film recommendations in the chapter on arts and educational films. We have not provided recommendations on instructional films since selection for those films would parallel what you select for the nonfiction print collection.

If your library collects entertainment films for its adult and child patrons, the argument for a teen feature film collection shouldn't be hard to make. Like any other group of patrons, teens have entertainment needs that your library should strive to satisfy. While the needs of teens could theoretically be satisfied by intermixing teen film selections with your children's or adult collection, you are less likely to attract teens to your library taking that approach.

If you experience resistance from your supervisors, administrators, or colleagues about the need for a teen collection, propose starting with a small collection to demonstrate that teens will use your library for entertainment. A smaller collection may require more advertising, face-out displays, and word-of-mouth marketing, but if you are careful to select your collection based on your community's input, this trial collection will definitely demonstrate the need.

If there is resistance from administration to providing money for even a small teen collection, consider preparing a proposal for your Friends of the Library group or a local service organization. Grant proposals are generally more attractive to foundations if you can partner with other community organizations. We have worked with local schools to get grant money for collection development; this could work for you as well, especially if you emphasize feature films that touch on social issues as well as arts and educational films.

Another way to stretch an inadequate budget is to put out requests to your teen patrons for donations of used movies. Many films now come with an added downloadable copy so that teens don't need the original DVD once they've downloaded the film. The patron has a legitimately purchased electronic copy and the library gets a DVD that's never been used. It's fiscally smart to suggest this to your teen patrons, even if you have a good budget.

Finally, if you lose the argument for a physically separate teen film collection, make sure that your adult collection contains films that appeal to teens. Then, make displays of films in your teen book collection area whenever possible. And try again at a later date.

ORGANIZING YOUR TEEN FILM COLLECTION

Teens are very aware that they are neither children nor adults. Therefore, a teen collection of any kind must be set apart in some way that distinguishes it from the larger collection. It does not have to be physically separated from the children's section, but the teens who use it must feel that the collection doesn't lump them in with the kids. On the other hand, teens have little desire to have their selections scrutinized by adults who might look down on or pass judgment on what they're choosing. Furthermore, an adult collection undoubtedly has a great deal of material of little interest to teens, and interfiling teen selections with adult selections makes it difficult for young adults to find what they want.

A teen collection that is set apart physically from adult and children's collections will be used more than one that is only distinguished from the adult or children's collections by its call numbers. Finding space may be a problem, but it isn't necessary to set your teen collection at a great distance from the others. A symbolic distinction, such as a separate aisle close to some comfortable seating or a wide aisle, can be enough. In our library, the end of the teen area closest to the public services desk is bordered by a row of spinning racks, which distinguish the area without blocking it off from casual supervision.

If you have an established teen book collection, it makes sense to place your teen film collection there as well. If your library has a single audiovisual department that contains all your films, use the same principles to make the teen area for films distinct and friendly for teens.

GENERAL GUIDELINES FOR SELECTING FILMS

You may be constrained by written or unwritten collection development rules to select films of superior quality. The rules may require more interpretation when applied to films for teens. A film aimed at teens may contain crude humor, for example, and could conceivably be rejected on that basis. That can be a mistake. Teens are more like Shakespeare's audiences, able to appreciate a mix of the earthy and the sublime.

Although you want to include the best films, there are mediocre films that teen viewers will enjoy and that may fill an emotional, developmental, or entertainment need as well. Films for an adult audience or older films may also resonate with teen viewers. Each viewer brings his or her own experience to watching a film just as a reader does, and a film or book that is of middling quality or that isn't obviously aimed at a teen audience may nonetheless inspire the imagination and satisfy the current emotional or entertainment needs of the viewer.

We've included more guidelines for selection in the individual chapters and sections, but the bottom line for building a teen feature film collection is to get input from teens in your community. Talk to your teens, listen to your teens, and act on what your teens say.

Remember that your teen patrons are without a doubt your best resource when looking for films to add to a teen collection. At the time of this writing, professional reviewers of entertainment videos and televisions series do not aim their reviews at a teen audience. Magazines and teen fan sites are essential for identifying potential candidates for purchase, but they don't answer all of the questions you as a librarian need to ask. Searching for reviews of anime online can sometimes prove frustrating, as sophisticated anime sites may refer to a title in Japanese only. You might find similar problems when searching for reviews of foreign films. To help combat this problem, we have tried to include the original titles of all recommended anime and foreign films in addition to the English titles.

We strongly suggest that selectors be as open to international films, animated films, and films with nontraditional heroes as today's teens are. Today's teens are more open than previous generations to sympathizing and identifying with characters that don't look, speak, or act exactly like themselves. International travel and having friends from other countries is not as unusual for the current generation of young adults than it was for earlier generations. So they are likely to feel strong connections to the world outside their hometown. They feel that they are part of the world community because today's technological interconnectivity gives them a larger perspective. Whereas past generations had to depend on the occasional correspondence with a pen pal or relative living abroad, teens today routinely correspond with members of a global community.

Purchasing international films and films with diverse casts can suitably resolve the issue of building a collection that features a wide range of ethnicities, religions, and races. Giving both sexes and all gender orientations fair treatment is often not as straightforward. Check your collection for sex and gender balance. Although teens may be able to identify with the identity quests of characters of the opposite sex or of different genders, there is still no reason not to offer films with strong characters of both sexes and a variety of sexual orientations and gender identities.

Teens are necessarily drawn to films that include teenage characters, but you can also include films with characters that are younger or older than your target audience if the characters are also facing questions of identity. For example, the 2004 film *Garden State*, starring Zach Braff and Natalie Portman, features 20-something characters struggling to find themselves. Make an effort to collect films that offer *characters* in a range of age groups, as well as films that appeal to *patrons* in a range of age groups. For instance, popular action/adventure films that appeal to adults will most likely also appeal to teens. Having duplicates of titles in different collections (adult versus teen versus junior) is not a new idea. Many adult books, such as *The Awakening* by Kate Chopin and *Invisible Man* by Ralph Ellison, have been included in teen collections or on teen reading lists for years. In fact, many books that are now thought of as young adult or even children's, such as *The Adventures of Huckleberry Finn* by Mark Twain or *Catcher in the Rye* by J. D. Salinger, were written for adults. Great books are great books at any age.

There are series aimed at adults that also appeal to teens because of their heroes, who may not be great role models but are just fun to watch or imagine being like. The following are examples of action/adventure series worth considering for your collection; be sure to include copies of older films in any movie series that is still generating new films:

- *Bourne* trilogy. Based on the Robert Ludlum books, amnesiac ex-CIA assassin Jason Bourne, played by Matt Damon, struggles to stay alive long enough to find out who he is.
- *Die Hard* series. Wisecracking New York City cop and loose cannon John McClane, played by Bruce Willis, battles terrorists.
- *Indiana Jones* series. Archaeologist and adventurer Indiana Jones, played by Harrison Ford, goes treasure hunting to prevent valuable objects from falling into the wrong hands.
- *James Bond* series. Based on Ian Fleming's books, James Bond is the ultimate spy.
- *The Mummy* series. Set in the 1920s through the 1940s, a librarian, her brother, and an adventurer set out to protect the world from ancient evils.
- *Pirates of the Caribbean* trilogy. A swashbuckling fantasy story of pirate Captain Jack Sparrow, played by Johnny Depp.
- *Star Wars* series. George Lucas's mythic space opera of good and evil played out through a multigenerational family epic.

TECHNOLOGY AND FORMAT

We are in a time of constant technological change, and though making predictions about the future of technology in home entertainment might seem foolish, it is necessary. The best way for you to choose the technology to offer is to ask your teen patrons what format they prefer when viewing films. The technological savvy of teen patrons will help you make your format decisions, as will the cost of library materials and the cost of the media players your patrons can afford. Teen patrons are often aware of what films are available before almost anyone else, and as such they may provide invaluable input to a librarian building a teen film collection; however, if economic constraints prevent teens from viewing films in the format a library has chosen, your film collection will basically be rendered worthless.

A recent trend that teens are spearheading is moving from being strictly consumers of films, music, and books to being creators and distributors using the power of readily available consumer electronics. If you talk to and team up with the teens that use your library, you and your collection will be on the leading edge of the technology wave.

The majority of teenagers are knowledgeable about existing technology and hot tech toys and tools. This is true in part because technology companies often aim their advertising at teens, but also in part because of the power of word-of-mouth among teens.

Today's generation of teens grew up never knowing a world without computers and the Internet; as a result, they think, communicate, and play differently than teenagers of previous generations. While they may be consumers of information and entertainment produced by corporations like everyone else, they are also creating and disseminating information and entertainment for themselves. In a sense, we are seeing a return to the time of homemade entertainment before radio and the phonograph, when everyone created their own entertainment for themselves and for each other.

It is very easy for adults to forget that teens lack the experience and patience that adults accumulate over time. Since many teens aren't aware of the many technological developments that have taken place in order to make present day products possible, they are often impatient with failings in technology. They also tend not to fully appreciate how much learning and unlearning it has taken to develop and market the technology that they've always had, nor the amount of money and research necessary to make said technology affordable and available for common use. The current technological climate is the norm for teens and the technology they don't remember is often considered ancient and irrelevant.

Teens still need to leave home to watch a first run Hollywood film (legally), but they also expect it to come out on cable and DVD (Digital Video Disc) quickly and cheaply. Television continues to be an important source of entertainment for the current generation of teens, even now, when the Internet, DVDs, and CDs are viable alternatives. Cable television and dish networks have markedly increased program selection and variety of offerings. Baby boomers remember when there were only three program choices during a set prime time. Today, one hour of the day or night is as likely to be as prime for viewing as any other. The need to fill up hundreds of channels means that even the most obscure films and television shows may be available at some time during a week or month. Because of increased awareness of previously inaccessible programs and films, and the ease of Internet advertising and online auctioning, it has become profitable for media companies to release rare, obscure, and many times forgettable materials in limited numbers. In addition, the Internet has broken down many of the informational barriers that previously made sales and distribution of non-mainstream films difficult, and potential viewers are now able to discover, research, and buy obscure films on a whim. The market for films has become more efficient in many ways, and cult or niche movies need not fall out of print, so long as there is a constant albeit small demand for them.

Videotapes and DVDs make it possible for everyone to adjust movie and television viewing to their own schedules, rather than according to the schedules imposed by corporations in New York or Los Angeles. DVRs (Digital Video Recorders) such as TiVo® allow people to save and play programs and movies at their own convenience and with a minimum of effort, especially compared to the once popular videocassette recorders (VCRs), which were a great advance in their time.

YouTube and other video sharing Web sites now offer the capacity to upload and view very short films and snippets of film for little to no cost, and these can be seen anywhere and by anyone in the world. Thus, as mentioned previously, teens have an outlet for their creativity that can be easily viewed by their peers, so they have moved from being exclusively consumers of films to creating their own. This is arguably the most significant result of recent advances in audiovisual technology, and perhaps the one with the heaviest impact on teens. If today's young adults and those in the future create their own films and share them with the global community, the face of entertainment in the future is going to be markedly different from what we can even imagine now. Distribution of self-made films has become very simple, and word-of-mouth or viral e-mail marketing can make hundreds of thousands of viewers aware of films. Teens have been creating content through "blogs" (weblogs, or online text diaries) for quite a while now and the next logical step is "vlogging" (video weblogging). As both teen cinematic experience and the resulting film sophistication grow, we can expect that out of the huge number of small works currently being made, classics will emerge, and the basis for mature works of genius will be laid down.

As a result of technological advances, today's teens have an abundance of choices for entertainment, and they are therefore likely to develop esoteric tastes. For example, we are likely to see repeats of phenomena such as the growth of Japanese animated films (anime) in the future. Although anime is now considered mainstream for both teenagers and adults, it was never a given or even likely that American teens would become such devoted fans of anime. Many factors contributed to the rise of anime in North America from a small cult of enthusiasts to a major segment of the film industry. Cable companies needed content to fill programming hours, while the Internet was able to put individuals with niche interests together, letting them share information about their favorite films and where to get them. The quality of anime and the appeal of its exotic nature to teens were big factors as well. Before anime was available generally in North America, fans recorded the original Japanese-language videos and added their own dubbing and subtitling in order to share them with friends; Japanese animated film then came to influence American film when teenage anime fans moved into the industry. The phenomenon of anime is now being repeated on a smaller scale for thousands of teen interests and is bringing specialist interests into popular culture

TRYING NEW FORMATS

Teens and new technology are a natural combination. Getting the newest technology in general and for entertainment in particular is the obvious choice to teens who don't have the old technology Teens generally rely on their parents to purchase the newest devices for playing films, so watch advertising around gift-giving seasons, including graduation, to see what's being rolled out.

At the time of writing, the battle between the two high definition optical disc formats, HDTV and Blu-ray has been decided in Blu-ray's favor. This was an unfortunate decision for librarians because Blu-ray discs store their information in the surface layer. Scratches that are minor and repairable in CDs and DVDs can make a Blu-ray disc unreadable and irreparable. In general, however, libraries have avoided making the decision about which high definition format to select, so details on how to deal with a collection of Blu-ray discs are hard to find. It may be necessary for a second generation of Blu-ray discs to come around before libraries become heavily invested in the format. Or librarians may decide that replacing damaged Blu-ray discs more often than they replaced DVDs is a price of business.

This doesn't mean that librarians should avoid trying new formats. A small collection of any new format is worth trying as long as it represents a small percentage of your budget and requires a minimal effort on the part of your technical services department. The authors' library, for example, has created a small teen collection of UMDs (Universal Media Discs) that can be played on PlayStation Portable systems. The collection is small at only about 20 copies, and though it is extremely popular for its size, with a high turnover rate, it also has a high theft and breakage rate. Demand for UMDs continues, but it has stabilized. The collection has been sufficient to meet a demand that has leveled off. The library is carrying out a similar experiment with Blu-ray discs for the teen collection.

If you're building a teen collection, you have to be especially bold when trying to keep up with patrons' format choices. On the one hand, your instincts (and your administrator) may tell you that a new format is too expensive for the number of uses it will get. On the other hand, you may believe the materials you buy will have a high circulation rate before the items wear out or disappear. Take a chance and spend a limited amount of money on a new format—it will probably last longer than you fear it will. Teens will likely appreciate the option and you may find that the risk is low enough and the interest is high enough to justify expanding the collection.

TECHNICAL SERVICES AND NEW FORMATS

Remember that buying items in a new format is not necessarily the end of the story when making those items available to your teen patrons. A new format usually involves some difference in package preparation for the rigors of circulation. Keep your technical services department informed of any proposed experiments with new formats. Springing new formats on them without informing or consulting with them may strain your working relationship.

If you're keeping up with teens, it is quite likely that the teen collection will be where new movie formats will first be purchased and decisions about how to catalog and package them will first be made. You and your technical services department need to work together on how the new format will be packaged and how it will be protected by your security system. Inform the selectors for both the adult and children's collections that you are negotiating how to handle a new format, and you may get useful input from them to help prevent the need for changes later on if they decide to start a similar collection. Decisions on physical processing, cataloging and classification, security, and shelving a new format depends on local precedents for similar formats more than on any generalized rules for new formats.

When you are trying a new format to see if it will be popular in your library, choose titles that have broad appeal, such as recent blockbusters, so that even if the format is a flop, you can still get a lot of use from the items you've bought. One way to help make sure that the items you select are of high interest is to check the OCLC (Online Computer Library Center) catalog to see what titles other libraries have.

An added benefit of checking OCLC to assist in deciding what to buy is that your catalogers won't have to create original bibliographic records, which will speed up the process of getting the items on the shelves. If you are beginning a collection in a new format and some or all of your selections are not in OCLC, be prepared for delays in cataloging. The new format may require that your technical services department investigate and interpret current MARC (Machine-Reading Cataloging) format and cataloging rules.

THE FUTURE OF FORMATS

Although the victor in the battle between high-definition DVD formats has been declared, this has by no means led to a slowdown in production of standard DVDs. High-definition DVDs work best for films that deserve high definition treatment and that are played on large screens. The films that cram special effects and hundreds of actors onscreen cry out for high-definition treatment on a large screen, and you can be assured that teens will watch them on a large screen when they can. However, teens also watch movies on laptops and other portable devices that can't display the detail available on a high-definition disc. If Blu-ray becomes more durable, or the price drops so low as to make the discs disposable, then not being able to catch the detail on portable devices won't matter. Until then, Blu-ray is likely to be a niche market geared toward playing epic, detailed movies on large screens, and conventional DVDs will continue to be a major part of the market. On the other hand, do keep in mind that teens will likely still play Blu-ray discs on their non-portable PlayStation 3 machines, so consider purchasing a Blu-ray copy of a title that you own multiple copies of in conventional DVD format.

It seems likely that digital films that can be downloaded to any type of device will eventually be the norm, but in the meantime, bandwidth for downloading and storage space for digital files both pose considerable constraints on extensive use. Consequently, short films and video clips have become massively popular through video sharing sites, and are fast becoming standard methods for sharing information or entertainment, provided it is only a few minutes long.

Ultimately, libraries need to keep all their options open. A library needs to keep collecting traditional DVDs, which are relatively durable. Meanwhile, they should also collect high-definition discs for the special effects-heavy blockbusters. And finally, libraries would be wise to invest in access to downloadable digital films in order to cater to multiple platforms and to provide continuous access to the film collection.

It is possible that sometime in the future, digital downloads of films will be quick, easy, and high-definition, but that future does not appear to be on the immediate horizon, and may even in the long run elude us.

In the meantime, physical formats are likely to play a significant role as a convenient way to carry or store high definition films to be played on large screen devices, or in situations where download speeds are a constraint. However, though they may not be perfected yet, digital downloads are nonetheless a convenient way to watch disposable movies on the go. At the time of writing, several major television network Web sites had begun distributing downloadable television episodes that can be watched on personal computers. Apple's iTunes and Amazon's Video on Demand (VOD) are among the video download sites pioneering the commercial distribution of videos.

A common approach to creating collections of digital media for libraries is to pool resources in consortia. Since there is no need to house physical copies of a film, and distribution is only limited by bandwidth, sharing resources in this way is an obvious choice. If there is going to be a problem in the future, it will likely occur when the demand for digital media becomes high for popular titles, copies of which can only be checked out by one person at a time. When hold queues become a problem, individual libraries will want to provide copies for their patrons. This may result in the breakup of some consortia if better-funded libraries decide that their patrons would be better served if the library went it alone. The question of how to provide interlibrary loan for downloadable media would be daunting.

VIDEOGAMES AND FILMS

A trend that may indicate a major shift in films is the increasing crossover between films and video games. Improvements in the technology of computer generating imaging (CGI) are equally applied in filmmaking and video game creation, particularly since a significant percentage of video games are based on films, and vice versa. Films that are based on videogames have traditionally met with little critical success, but usually have great popular appeal. The *Lara Croft: Tomb Raider* films are perhaps the most familiar example of the crossover from video game to film. These films and games demonstrate how a successful idea in one sector of entertainment can become the basis for making a profit in the other.

Movies have always had ties to other forms of media, usually merchandise tie-ins that are sold to generate profit. These types of tie-in products include soundtracks and videogames that are released at the same time as the film as part of a general public relations campaign. Video games may even be released with DVD copies of the films they are based on.

The connections and even the boundaries between films and video games may become more muddled in the future and result in a hybrid media. Books, magazines, and films are media that one views passively unless one writes in the margins, writes letters to the editor, or heckles the screen. The Internet allows users to make choices about where to go using hyperlinks, and increasingly the boundaries among consumers of content, direct participants, and creators of content are breaking down.

Ideas that increase interactivity are now being applied in videogames. Wireless controllers such as those in Wii videogames enable players to interact in games in more precise and controlled ways so that even the motions of face muscles have the potential for being tracked and mirrored on avatars within games.

Second Life is in effect a videogame that is played on the Internet without competitive rules. Participants are free to build homes or businesses and interact in a sort of face-to-face manner. Ultimately, films may become similarly interactive while video games have the potential to add plots in the sports, romance, or mystery genres. Interesting trends are all around, but the outcome is very much uncertain, and whether libraries will collect such hybrids or provide access to them is only conjecture. Fascinating conjecture, but conjecture.

Today's teens manipulate existing videogames to become creators rather than just consumers. A new kind of self-made film genre has evolved from the improved graphics of games and is called *machinima*, a combination of the words "machine" and "cinema." Machinima is the phenomenon of video created by photographically capturing scenes from a game as it is played, and then creating a new story that is scripted and edited by the machinima creator, or "machinimator." Gamers have developed ways to script their own films by manipulating the game world. Some of the best-known examples of machinima are the *Red vs. Blue* videos, which use characters from the Xbox videogame *Halo*. The Academy of Machinima Arts & Sciences (http://www.machinima.org), founded in 2002 by Paul Marino and others, holds festivals and awards "Mackies" to the best examples of the genre.

Machinima makes use of existing videogames' graphics to create new films. The advances in technology available to teens make it likely that they will be increasingly patching together film, animation, and their own imagination to create videogames from the ground up. Once again, the trends are there for all to see, but the final outcome is excitingly unclear.

2

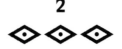

GETTING TEENS INVOLVED

It can't be said often enough that your teen patrons are your best resource regarding teen films. However, getting suggestions from teens who already use the library is only the first step in building a great teen film collection. In this chapter you'll find out how to stimulate teen interest by catching the much sought after attention of this group of patrons. Teens rely on the opinions of the their circle of friends for both positive and negative advice on what to watch, read, or listen to, and this chapter offers tips on how to make your film collection the hottest buzz in town.

GETTING TEENS TO TALK TO YOU

A study done in 2005 by the Pew Internet & American Life Project indicated that young adults are using libraries today more than ever.[1] While this is excellent news, many librarians are nonetheless running into difficulty discovering ways to give young adult patrons more of a voice in determining what materials their library should collect. Like everyone else, young adults are busy people, and catching their attention is not an easy task. Here are some ways to connect with these patrons:

- Create a page on your library's web site devoted strictly to teens, with instructions on how to find films in the catalog and how to place holds on films. Use this page to showcase new films and film-related materials, periodicals, and Web sites. Provide a way for teens to post a simple 1 to 5 star rating scale on films, or run a contest every month for teens that post a review. Do a random drawing of the names of the reviewers and reward them with a small gift certificate to the local cinema or retail film store.

- Try providing a unique way for teen patrons to post quick reviews. A good model for this kind of activity might be The Four Word Movie Review, which is an entire movie review that consists of four words. You could also challenge the teens to write their film reviews as *haiku*. Reducing a film review to a select number of words is challenging and teens may find it fun as well. A great way to learn the opinions of your teen film watchers is to provide comment sheets and patron request forms in the area the video collection is housed.

- Running periodic in-house surveys about teens' favorite films can be enlightening. Hold contests asking teens to vote for their favorite film and have a draw for voters to win a DVD of a current popular film as the prize.

- Establish a special collection of books and magazines on films and filmmaking. A good list of choices can be found in Chapter 7 of this book.

- Target teen film fans by establishing groups that discuss or view certain categories of films, such as an anime and manga club or a "Books into Films" group.

- Create filmographies, either as handy bookmarks or as pathfinders that relate to a new film when it is released. Examples of appropriate filmographies might include films with the same actor, films by the same director, and movie tie ins. Simple genre lists are helpful as well.

- Create focused sub-collections for television programs, independent films, anime, documentaries, or horror. If your collection is big enough, feel free to create other sub-collections.

- Create tester collections based on new formatting such as high definition Blu-ray DVDs or Universal Media Discs.

- Work with your local schools to advertise library film programs. Ask art teachers if their students can create special posters to advertise upcoming film programs. Ask writing teachers if their students can write a review of a film watched in the library or the classroom.

- Create an information e-mail list for teen film fans so you can send out information on new titles or upcoming programs.

PROGRAMMING

There are few things harder for librarians who cater to young adults than creating programs and activities that establish the library as a place for young adults to gather and hang out. As librarians are aware, libraries serve many, many functions in our community, but one that is increasingly being recognized as central is that of community center. Places where teens can just be teens without being considered nuisances are limited in most communities. Teen film programming lets the library serve teen patrons in ways that only libraries can.

Teens love films and enjoy watching them with other teens who love films. With the creation of video sharing Web sites like YouTube, it should come as no surprise that this is the age of do-it-yourself video creation and sharing. Creating activities for teen movie lovers can bring some unique and fresh programming that bring teens to the table.

Films and teens are a match made in heaven. Teens have been a huge part of film audiences since the 1950s. According to the 2006 United States Movie Attendance Study of the Motion Picture Association of America, during the years 2004 to 2006, 28 percent of filmgoers were in the age range of 12 to 24 years old. In 2006, 85 percent of the 20 top grossing films were either PG or PG 13 films. This is good news for libraries that want to hold film-screening events.

However, there are a few important guidelines for creating a teen film program. Film programs geared towards teens can sometimes call for higher end audiovisual equipment than is standard in most public librar-ies. A large screen television, or the ability to project on to a large screen, is almost a necessity if the audience size is over 10 to 15 people. Also, remember that to screen a film for an audience at a library, public perfor-mance rights must be obtained unless the library has purchased a public performance copy of the title in question.

Obtaining a Public Performance License

It is relatively easy to obtain public performance rights to screen a single film and usually a phone call to one of the three major licensing companies listed below will get you what you need. Various factors like the size of the audience may affect the fee and are best discussed with the licensing companies. Blanket licenses that cover a number of film studios may be a better option if your library screens films on a regular basis. For libraries, the fees for a blanket license are usually based on the number of active library patrons. The major firms that handle these licenses include:

Movie Licensing USA

Schools http://www.movlic.com/k12/siteLicense.html

Libraries http://www.movlic.com/library/index.html

Movie Licensing USA is a division of Swank Motion Pictures, Inc.
  http://www.swank.com

(800) 876 5577

Criterion Pictures

http://www.criterionpicusa.com

(800) 890 9494

A helpful FAQ sheet on copyright issues is available from Criterion Pictures Canada. http://www.criterionpic.com/CPL/lcl_faqonpp.html

Facets Video

http://www.facets.org/asticat

(800) 532 2387

A division of Facets

Multi-Media, Inc., Facets Media is one of the nation's largest distributors of foreign, classic, cult, art, and hard to find cinema.

Motion Picture Licensing Corporation (MPLC)

http://www.mplc.com

(800) 462 8855

This resource is used by a large number of libraries and has a diverse
  number of titles.

The Motion Picture Association of America and the American Library
Association should have all the information necessary to clear up any
remaining questions programmers may have. Naturally, the United States
Copyright Office is the ultimate authority on copyright issues.

Popular Film Screenings

Running the first films in a series like *Spider-Man* when a later film in the
series has just been released in cinemas always has great program potential. Additionally, screening a film that had a limited theatrical release
can bring to the library fans who missed seeing it on a larger screen. This
applies most specifically to fans of anime, documentaries, or foreign film
titles. Serving free popcorn and soda can add to the ambience and the
general movie viewing experience. For a film with die-hard fans, try offering related activities like a trivia contest or a cosplay (costume play) event,
where fans dress up as their favorite characters. Cosplay is highly evolved

within the anime and manga fan base, but is also now becoming popular with fans of American films and books. Some dedicated gamers are dressing up for film events as their favorite game character or even as the avatar they use when playing MMORPGs, which are Massively Multi-Player Online Role Playing Games. A film like *The Rocky Horror Picture Show* is a well-known example of a film event to which audiences generally come in costume.

Film Festivals and Marathons

Film festivals that feature the work of certain actors or directors can generate unique teen film events. Consider a day-long marathon on days when there is no school, or around the holidays. Tying holidays in with films is always fun. Screening anti-holiday films is even more fun. The film titles below are a few holiday and anti-holiday titles your teen patrons may enjoy.:

Halloween

Donnie Darko (2001) R

> This movie takes place over Halloween, and the giant rabbit that stalks Donnie appears to be wearing a Halloween costume. Or is it real?

Halloween (1978) R

> In 1963, six-year-old Michael Myers killed his sister on Halloween. Fifteen years later, he escapes from the mental institution he's been confined in and heads home to kill again.

Halloween (2007) R

> Rob Zombie's remake of the John Carpenter classic horror film.

Thanksgiving

Pieces of April (2003) R

> April Burns (played by Katie Holmes) invites all of her family and friends for a Thanksgiving celebration that may be her ill mother's last.

Christmas

Christmas Vacation (1989), PG-13

> The Griswold family of National Lampoon fame have a disastrous Christmas.

Gremlins (1984) PG-13

> A teen receives a unique pet for Christmas, which results in horrible Gremlins taking over the town.

Home Alone (1990) PG

> This holiday comedy about an 8-year-old left alone over Christmas has heavy nostalgia value for teens

The Nightmare Before Christmas (1993) PG

> This animated film by Tim Burton is the story of Jack Skellington, head of Halloweentown, who finds the way to Christmastown and kidnaps Santa.

Scrooged (1988) PG-13

> Bill Murray stars as a mean television executive in this take off of Dicken's *A Christmas Carol*.

Valentine's Day

Corpse Bride (2005) PG

> This Tim Burton film is the story of a Victorian-era arranged marriage between Victor Van Dort and Victoria Everglot that goes awry when the groom finds himself married to a corpse.

Eternal Sunshine of the Spotless Mind (2004) R

> When Joel breaks up with Clementine, he is heartbroken to learn that she has arranged to have her memories of their relationship deleted from her mind. When Joel decides to do the same, he realizes that he really does love her.

How to Lose a Guy in 10 Days (2003) PG-13

> An advertising executive bets that he can make a woman fall in love with him in 10 days, and his target is a reporter who is writing an article on how to lose a man in 10 days.

Groundhog Day

Groundhog Day (1993) PG-13

> In this Harold Ramis film, Bill Murray plays an unpleasant weatherman sent to Punxsutawney, Pennsylvania to cover the Groundhog Day event. He wakes the next morning only to find himself doomed to repeat the day over and over.

Hanukkah

Eight Crazy Nights (2002) PG-13

> *Eight Crazy Nights* is an animated musical comedy about Davey Stone, voiced by Adam Sandler, who gets arrested for theft and drunkenness and is released to his old sports referee.

Fourth of July

Born on the Fourth of July (1989) R

> *Born on the Fourth of July* is the story of Vietnam Vet Ron Kovic and how he becomes an antiwar activist.

Independence Day (1996) PG-13

> When aliens come to destroy Earth, the president and a small group of survivors must figure out how to stop them.

Prom Night

Carrie (1976) R

> Ostracized teen Carrie White finally succumbs to anger and uses her powers to destroy her tormentors at the prom.

Graduation

Graduation (2007) NR

> Four high school seniors decide to rob a bank on their graduation day.

Special Screenings at Local Movie Theaters

A great way to involve teens in film discussions is to join forces with a local movie theater and hold "A Book and a Movie" program. The theater can run a special showing for library patrons of a book-based film that is currently in theaters, and after the film is over, a discussion of the book/movie can be held right in the theater. The library, the movie house, and a local bookstore can jointly promote the event. Free related giveaways are always added incentives to attract a larger crowd.

Movie Discussion and Appreciation Programs

Encourage teens to start thinking critically about films. Most teen film fans have no formal or informal instruction on film appreciation. Bring in speakers on the history of film or on the basics of filmmaking as the first step in creating a knowledgeable fan base for historic or less mainstream films. Hold movie discussion programs in the library to help teens develop critical thinking skills. Bring in experts on screen writing, cinematography, film techniques, and animation. Finding local film experts may seem daunting at first, but area colleges may have professors teaching filmmaking courses who might be interested in giving a program, or may be willing to suggest a college student or group with the requisite skills. Local newspapers may have film critics on staff. Local television or cable television stations may be willing to hold a class at the library on the best ways to shoot videos for air on television. Local universities or technical schools that have classes on videography, cinematography, or screenplay writing can also be tapped as a resource.

Specialized Teen Advisory Boards

It is important that teens have a voice in what their library selects, and teen advisory boards are a great way to give them that voice. Consider establishing a general teen film advisory board, as well as advisory boards interested in specialized topics like anime, cult films, fantasy, television programs, or horror films.

A specialized teen advisory board for an anime collection, for example, can really benefit a library's film selectors. Anime fans are very devoted and can prove an incredible resource. Although most anime distributors have created their own ratings system that can be found on the packaging, there are sometimes surprises nonetheless. Consider sponsoring a teen anime advisory board that pre-screens non-rated and DVDs that have not been professionally reviewed in order to recommend where to shelve a film within the library.

Fantasy, science fiction, and cult film programs are unexplored new sources for teen programming. Fans love to get together to watch *Mystery Science Theater 3000*, a television show on which three characters are forced to watch terrible movies and end up spending the entire time heckling and poking fun of what is happening on the screen. Though the show is no longer airing new episodes, some of the original *Mystery Science Theater 3000* writers and performers are now releasing bad films with funny commentaries under the moniker *The Film Crew*. Part of the enjoyment of these underground films is the ability to quote them and be sure someone will get the joke: large audiences ensure that someone will.

Programs for Teen Filmmakers

One of the most popular film programs for teens in libraries is "Make Your Own Movie" contests. To offer your own version of this contest, establish an age range for participation, a maximum length for entries, and most importantly, what technological format the films must be in to qualify. Be prepared to prescreen all entries for appropriateness of material. New and exciting ideas on how to run teen film festivals are in the professional literature. You can find excellent and comprehensive information on teen film festivals in Susan Conlon's "Putting Your Teens in Focus With Films" in the August 2007 issue of *VOYA* magazine. Offer appropriate prizes for the winners, and don't forget to seek sponsors from the community to help underwrite and promote the festival.

As teens acquire the ability to make their own films, they also become interested in learning more out about filmmaking technology. Once your teen patrons begin making their own films, be sure to carry magazines and books on filmmaking technology. Think about pairing up with a local electronics store and holding a technology fair where experts demonstrate the latest electronic developments in the filmmaking field, or have the teens themselves run a program for their peers on what filmmaking equipment they use. As new technology for filmmaking evolves, becoming better and more affordable, teens will surely continue to be early adopters. For example, new digital film cameras are being created that achieve the quality of the present day conventional analog film cameras, but at a greatly reduced cost. The ability to create professional looking, theatrical grade films will likely become available and affordable to amateur filmmakers in the near future. A well-funded school or library, or schools and libraries in joint cooperation, may be able to acquire the newest technological devices and allow unprecedented access for student filmmakers to these cutting edge inventions.

Teen filmmakers will undoubtedly discover that technology is not enough, and will want to learn about techniques for making better films, so your film collection should go beyond the technology and include works on filmmaking in general.

Library Displays

Film collections are predominantly browsing collections. There are many ways to catch the attention of patrons and draw them in, including book and music tie-ins or a combination of posters and props. Creating an eye-catching display can be as simple as getting a tall director's chair and pairing it with an old-fashioned movie megaphone or old films reels. Discover what local stores usually have large cardboard displays or posters featuring newly released films, and ask the manager if the displays are ever given away to libraries or schools. Since displays often end up being thrown away, most stores are usually cooperative. Consider buying life-size cardboard figures of famous film characters like Darth Vader, who will never go out of popularity. Film posters are also relatively inexpensive and are readily accessible from many stores as well as on line. A line of framed posters on a wall near the teen film collection can attract attention from across the room. Be prepared to add new posters as new films come out. When new posters go on display, run a contest for teens to win the old posters. Posters always appeal to teens, and getting them from the library will create a positive response from teen patrons. Creative signage that utilizes appropriate fonts, photographs, and graphics is easily created on computers and has the added benefit of being relatively economical.

In summary, some of the programs that increase teen use of the library, like film discussion groups, are not very different from traditional patron programs. However, you can also take on the responsibility to provide programs that promote film literacy, film history, and film criticism, which are usually courses of study that a student does not encounter until college, if ever.

NOTE

1. "Teens and Technology: Youth are leading the transition to a fully wired and mobile nation." *PEW/Internet & American Life Project.* (July 27, 2005), http://www.pewinternet.org/

3

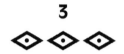

EXPLORING ISSUES
OF IDENTITY:
SUGGESTED FILMS

Stories that explore issues of identity are journeys of personal self-discovery, unique to the characters involved, and without a uniform goal. The goal of teen life, and consequently of teen films, is the struggle to define oneself. The search for one's own identity is very personal, and it is therefore impossible to know just which film or story will offer guidance or inspiration to a teen searching for his or her place in the world. A film doesn't have to be great or even good to provide tremendous value to a teenager; it will do so simply by answering the right questions for the teenager who sees it. We recommend many mediocre films that we know teens will love and learn from but that they will be embarrassed to remember liking when they're adults.

Overall, films that deal with issues of identity can be described as coming-of-age films and organized in many ways. We've chosen to organize our suggested films in three groups: "Who Am I?" films, "Lost in a Group" films, and "Other Cultures, Other Times" films. "Who Am I?" films involve self-discovery resulting from rites-of-passage or loss of innocence. "Lost in a Group" films involve joining or rejecting social groups as a way to explore identity. "Other Cultures, Other Times" films look at individuals from other cultures or identities that don't match the majority of American teens.

   A theme that appears in almost every film that deals with issues of identity is romance. The first thing a teen must discover about him or herself is whom he or she finds attractive. Traditionally, society expects a young person to be attracted to someone of the opposite sex who has a similar background. Before the last few decades, teens tended to have friends of the same sex and a romantic relationship with one person of the opposite sex. Teens today are comfortable being friends with members of the opposite sex as well as members of the same sex. Perhaps no other generation has had the freedom to just be friendly with almost anyone. Teens today have the opportunity to get to know other people (and themselves) without having to worry about how they look and what they say. Teens today socialize in groups that include both sexes and all backgrounds. Just like in *Pretty in Pink* (1986), a teen can go to the prom without a date.

   The idea of loving someone in a romantic sense is really part and parcel of "Who Am I?" films. Romances where boy meets girl occur in most teen films, but there are plenty of films that include boy meets boy or girl meets girl storylines. In the past, gay, bisexual, and transgender characters in films were uncommon and their stories did not end happily. In more recent films, happy endings are much more likely and teens can find characters like themselves, for whom having a love life does not doom them to punishment or death.

   The appeal of a romantic scene is not diminished when a romance is between members of the same sex. The girls in the anime club in our library found the romantic relationship between two male policemen in the anime series *Fake* adorable. Teenaged girls love lovers, whoever they might be. Teenaged boys are more uncomfortable about same-sex romance than girls are but they tend to be uncomfortable about romance in general.

   Another opportunity for teens today is to date people of different racial, ethnic, or religious backgrounds. Differences in social status, wealth, and education do not prevent teenagers from pursuing relationships.

   There are very few films for teens that can be described simply as romances, and the ones that do fit the description usually end tragically. Films such as *A Walk to Remember* (2002) that are based on romantic novels fit the category of romance and, typically, the girl dies in the end.

   The structure of a romance requires that two people in love develop their relationship in relative isolation. The more characters that get involved in the couple's relationship, the more comical and farcical the romance becomes. Teens and teenaged characters can't have relationships that don't involve family, friends, teachers, and busybodies in general. The romantic aspect of a teen's life is only part of his or her life and is affected by everyone and everything else around him or her.

Also, the traditional pattern of a romantic story usually ends with marriage and sometimes with the prospect of children. Most teens are not ready for those commitments.

"WHO AM I?" FILMS

In "Who Am I?" films, the protagonist faces a challenge or series of challenges and comes to learn about his or her identity through the experience. Some films show teens facing challenges that are typical rites of passage, such as:

- Dating or aspiring to date
- Hanging out where there are no adults or authority figures
- Sports or failure at sports
- School
- Dealing with a family that is embarrassing or boring

Other films, however, make use of challenges that are more unusual and unique, such as personal journeys toward maturity or dealing with loss.

The teenage years are often a time of suspense, where teens float between being children and being adults, and where both the past and the future seem alien and distant. Teens' bodies and relationships are new to them in ways that are both horrible and wonderful, as well as painful and joyful. Since their parents are no longer protecting them, each challenge or change in these years is a new one to teens They have no basis for understanding that their joy or pain in these situations is transitory and part of the human condition. Films can demonstrate the transitory nature of many of the feelings teenagers deal with. Many films offer helpful examples and advice on how to deal with both pain and happiness in mature ways. Films of self-discovery belong at the core of a teen collection.

Adolescence is a time for deeply philosophical as well as very mundane questions:

- Who am I?
- Can I live with who I am?
- What is my place in the universe?
- Am I normal?

- Do I want to be normal when I look at everyone around me?
- Will I ever find someone to love and that will love me?
- Will I ever stop being a virgin? When?

Many events in a teenager's life have more significance than they would for an adult, not only because teens may be experiencing these events for the first time, but also because many events have a significant impact on what is to come. Living a normal life can be either an adventure or an ordeal. Even boredom is more intense in teen films than in adult films because the characters suspect that they are forever doomed to lead boring lives.

An example of a "Who Am I?" film is one that many readers may have seen, the 1989 film *Dead Poets Society*. The characters in the film are typical prep school students facing typical prep school problems, such as balancing workload and extra curricular activities, finding the right crowd, and getting into the dating game—until they encounter an exceptional teacher who challenges the school's stultifying rules and rigid discipline. Heavily influenced by the teacher's idealism and subversive belief system, one teen character confronts his father with his decision to become an actor, and the ensuing conflict results in that character's suicide. The tragedy deeply affects the character's roommate, who develops the self-confidence to stand up to the school's authorities when the teacher is blamed for the suicide and subsequently fired.

Teens can recognize the injustice and prejudice that can emerge in a school that is unfair, unreasonable, and uninspiring (like the rest of the world). The members of the Dead Poets Society, an underground reading group the teacher establishes for his students, provides various characters for teens to empathize and identify with. Although it is a group that meets apart from other students, the Society is not a tribe to be broken out of, but rather a group that provides support for each individual's quest for identity.

The "Who Am I?" film is not so much a guide to self-discovery as it is proof that self-discovery is possible.

"LOST IN A GROUP" FILMS

"Lost in a Group" teen films feature characters who are initially defined by the groups they belong to. These films document the journeys through which these characters are taught or learn to see individuals where they previously saw undifferentiated members of a larger group.

In urban and suburban high schools, teens often end up in "tribes" or cliques, sometimes by choice and other times as a result of peer pressure. Aligning oneself with a tribe can be very helpful for a teen who is developing his or her personal identity; the tribe serves as a metaphoric skeleton for that young person's sense of self, providing both support and structure, almost like a trellis does for a growing vine. Naturally, what constitutes a tribe can vary significantly from era to era and place to place, but some examples of tribes include Goths, jocks, stoners, fashionistas, brainiacs, and cheerleaders.

Teens distinguish themselves from other teens by what they wear, the type of music they listen to, the games they play, or the cult films they watch. By choosing to be part of a tribe, young people have the luxury of establishing an identity and differentiating themselves from others without running the risk of isolation. Those who belong to the tribe may be different from everybody else, but they are all different together, generally by choice. Unfortunately, choice is not always a factor. Teenagers also risk being assigned to a tribe by others who pigeonhole them based on their interests, looks, or degree of popularity.

Films often explore identity by bringing together teens from different tribes so that they can discover the common humanity beneath the stereotypes. The concept of tribes can also be exploited for shallow humor when the stereotypes aren't challenged and are instead exposed as facades. The classic film about teens that have been stereotyped but end up discovering both themselves and one another is the 1985 John Hughes film *The Breakfast Club*. At the beginning of the film, each of the five main characters is defined solely as a high school stereotype. They are referred to as the princess, the criminal, the brain, the athlete, and the basket case. Over the course of the film, however, these five individuals slip out from behind their stereotypes and learn to see each other as human beings. They discover that, in every case, each one is more than just the label that he or she has been given.

The director of *The Breakfast Club*, John Hughes, was so successful at creating a new category of film that his are usually the first films that come to mind when the term "teen film" is used. For adults who grew up in the 1980s or earlier, they are often the *only* films that come to mind. Starting with his directorial debut, the 1984 teen film *Sixteen Candles*, Hughes returned over and over again to the theme of teenagers struggling to discover themselves and their individuality; this theme continued in *The Breakfast Club*, which centered on an issue many teens face—the dilemma of not wanting to stand out, but also of wanting to be special, if not unique.

A selection of John Hughes's films is included in the list of recommendations based on their status as classic films.

John Hughes's films are characteristic of teen films made in the 1980s and early 1990s. The 2004 film *Mean Girls* is an outstanding example of a modern teen film, fully aware of its cinematic history and yet telling a contemporary story. Adapted from Rosalind Wiseman's 2002 adult nonfiction book, *Queen Bees & Wannabes: Helping Your Daughter Survive Cliques, Gossip, Boyfriends, and Other Realities of Adolescence*, and written by *Saturday Night Live* writer and cast member, Tina Fey, the film is reminiscent of many of the John Hughes films. The main character is Cady Heron, a fish out of water transfer student who has been home schooled in Africa and is suddenly thrown into an American high school in which the teens are divided into cliques. The film begins with Cady being adopted by the outcast group who decide to teach the trendy rich girls (the Plastics) a lesson. But Cady is seduced into becoming one of the Plastics before she remembers her own standard of ethics. Ultimately, she returns to her senses and proceeds to remind everyone in the school to value their uniqueness and individuality. The film is not as sappy as it sounds. At the end, the viewer sees Cady's fantasy about a new generation of Plastics getting hit by a school bus.

The eponymous main character in the 2004 film *Napoleon Dynamite* is a modern antihero, a tribe of one, who is so unaware of his high school's social hierarchy that he might as well have been home schooled in Africa like *Mean Girls'* Cady. Napoleon lives in Preston, Idaho, where he doesn't fit into any conceivable group. The interesting thing about his character is that he rarely seems to notice his status as a social outsider and therefore rarely seems bothered by it. He just lives his life and ultimately stumbles into becoming more than he seems, to both his classmates and the film's audience. At the end of the film, Napoleon manages to help his friend Pedro, another outsider, win an election for class president over the stereotypical popular girl by disco dancing in front of the student body in a Pedro For President t-shirt. He is so oblivious to the idea that he should care about fitting into a group, and so spectacularly out of the ordinary, that in the end everyone ends up rooting for Napoleon and Pedro to succeed. After watching this film, teens can appreciate that the philosophy of just being oneself might work for them as well.

"OTHER CULTURES, OTHER TIMES" FILMS

"Other Cultures, Other Times" films show teens the differences and commonalities of growing up in different cultures and times. An added benefit of this category of films is that they allow more teens to see people on the big screen who look and act like them. At one time, the protagonists in a film had to be of European descent for a Hollywood film to be a hit in America. This is no longer the case. Teens are now comfortable watching films from around the world, with heroes of any nationality, of either sex, of any faith, and of any gender. These films often explore the process of finding one's identity, but do so in cultures and places with which the majority of American teens are unfamiliar.

This openness to foreign films is a fairly recent change for the entire American market. Distributors were unlikely to expect any foreign film to be a commercial success in the past, but as more material was needed in Hollywood, and the American public showed its willingness to watch foreign films, these movies became more available and commonly viewed in America. For a variety of reasons, including the expanding global community, the growth of the Internet, and an increase in world travel by teens, young people are especially open to appreciating films from around the world.

In the 1950s, when Hollywood first began marketing films to teens, the teen characters in films were primarily middle class and always white Americans; now, both independent and mainstream Hollywood films often include ethnic characters or nontraditional heroes and heroines. Today more teens can see their own faces, as well as the faces of their friends and family, in films.

A film that falls nicely into the "Other Cultures, Other Times" category is the 1998 German film *Run, Lola, Run*. We get an insight into the current Germany that is not like the image we usually get in American films, and is familiar and strange in unexpected ways. The films opens with a phone call to Lola from her boyfriend, Manni, who tells her that he has lost 100,000 Deutsche Marks of a drug dealer's money. Lola has 20 minutes to get more money and take it across town to save his life. Lola drops the phone, but when the camera pans through the room to the television, the audience sees a cartoon Lola on the screen, running down the stairs. The viewer immediately recognizes that time and narrative are going to unwind in unexpected ways in this film. Lola fails in her first attempt to save Manni's life, but the story starts all over again, and Lola has several chances to change her actions, altering the ultimate outcome for herself, Manni, and everyone else she meets.

Run, Lola, Run is about making decisions and dealing with the consequences until you get it right. By way of comparison, in two similar American films where the teen protagonists deal with time and fate, the 2001 film *Donnie Darko* and the 2004 film *The Butterfly Effect*, the heroes' decisions and actions make their situations worse as order descends into chaos. The results are tragic. In *Run, Lola, Run,* however, Lola's actions create both good and bad consequences for the characters she encounters; cinematic snapshots cleverly expose their fates. But for Lola and Manni, the ultimate result is a happy ending, as chaos becomes order.

Run, Lola, Run is a terrific film at first viewing, but it is so filled with glimpses of untold stories and puzzles that it bears repeated viewings. At one point, Lola climbs into an ambulance and holds a dying man's hand, saving him. She is running for her lover's life, but still she stops to comfort a stranger. The frantic chase is interspersed with scenes from Lola's ordinary life where the viewer learns more about her and the other characters.

This German film moves at a breakneck pace with a tight, driving soundtrack and a definite taste of the surreal. One clever critic called it a "rave fairy tale." However you wish to describe or categorize it, it has become a cult classic for American teens. Although it resembles an American independent film in some ways, it has a different feel that marks it as not American, and is very refreshing for that reason.

WHAT TO LOOK FOR WHEN SELECTING

- When looking at films, remember that many classic films that deal with identity issues can appeal to teens whether the films were originally marketed to teens or not.
- The search for self includes a lot of embarrassing moments, and some of those involve crude humor, so don't reject a film based only on its crudity. Seeing the worst that can happen to someone and imagining it for yourself can often be cathartic.
- Be open to films with nontraditional heroes, films from around the world, and films produced by independent studios.
- Make sure your collection caters to both your male and female teen patrons. Teens may be able to identify with the identity quests of the opposite sex, but that is no reason not to offer a selection of teen films featuring both strong male and strong female characters. Be open to characters that don't fit the traditional male or female gender roles as well.
- Consider including films with characters who are facing questions of identity but who are younger or older than your teen patrons.
- Don't forget to talk to your teen patrons and listen to their suggestions as a necessary part of identifying titles for your collection.

"ISSUES OF IDENTITY" FILMS

8 Mile (2002) R

> Rapper B-Rabbit, as played by real life rap artist Eminem, struggles with his life and music career in Detroit. As expected, this film has a great rap soundtrack.

10 Things I Hate About You (1999) PG-13

> This is Shakespeare's *The Taming of the Shrew* set in a modern day American high school. Sophomore Bianca is forbidden to date until her older sister Katarina does; to get around this, Bianca's suitors hire an upperclassman to romance Katarina. This is a perennially popular film with teens.

12 and Holding (2005) R

> With some genuinely funny moments, this film tackles the crushing problems of being a kid today. Three friends come to terms with life and each other after an incident in which one friend's twin is killed in a fire set by local bullies.

13 Going on 30 (2004) PG

> In this sweet romp a young girl wishes she was big, gets her wish, and ultimately learns that being big is not what she really wants.

16 Candles (1984) R

> When Samantha's birthday coincides with her sister's wedding, the family doesn't even remember Samantha's birthday. In the meantime, a crazy freshman tries to seduce Samantha when her heart already belongs to senior hunk Jake. John Hughes's directorial debut is a teen classic, though most teens won't recognize what a turning point it represents.

All Quiet on the Western Front (1930) PG Black and white
All Quiet on the Western Front (1979) NR Made for television

> The classic black and white version of Erich Maria Remarque's novel is still as powerful and moving as when it was released in 1930. The film tells the story of a young German student who is encouraged to enlist in the military by a teacher and comes of age in the World War I trenches. The television remake might be more accessible and attractive to contemporary teen viewers.

All the Real Girls (2003) R

> When Noel returns home from boarding school to her small town in North Carolina instead of going to college, she falls for Paul, a local womanizer who is also her older brother's best friend. Paul has dated half of the girls in town, but in the end, he discovers that Noel is the one he truly cares for.

Almost Famous (2000) R

> This film is director Cameron Crowe's tribute to his early days as a writer for *Rolling Stone* magazine. Set in the 1970s, this film tells the story of

15-year-old William Miller, a high school student sent by *Rolling Stone* on a road trip with up and coming rock band Stillwater. This is an extraordinary coming of age film for nearly every one of the characters.

American Graffiti (1973) PG
More American Graffiti (1979) PG

In the original, George Lucas's homage to American teenagers, the action takes place over the course of one night in 1962. The night of a dance, just before two of the characters go off to college, a group of teens go through individual journeys that change their lives. Music plays a prominent role in the action and unifies the movie. The sequel continues the stories of the main characters on four different days during the 1960s.

American Me (1992) R

Santana, a teenage Hispanic gang member, is sent to prison for 18 years, where he learns to be a hardened criminal. This hard and bitter story shows what minority and underprivileged teens face growing up in Los Angeles or any large American city.

ATL (2006) PG-13

Seventeen-year-old Rashad hangs with his friends at an Atlanta roller skating rink. With a great rap soundtrack backed up by some amazingly choreographed roller skating scenes, this film is about teens struggling through life, getting by, and growing up.

Beautiful Thing (1996) R United Kingdom

In this beautiful and human story, two 16-year-old boys fall in love with each other in contemporary South East London.

Before Sunrise (1995) R
Before Sunset (2004) R

Jessie, an American bumming around Europe, meets Celine, a French student, on a train. They form an almost instantaneous emotional bond, and decide to spend 14 hours together in Vienna. In the sequel, the pair meets again, nine years later. The same actors, Ethan Hawke and Julie Delpy, star in both films, and the second film is just as enjoyable as the first.

Better Luck Tomorrow (2002) R

This film tells the story of a group of Asian American teens who seem to have it all—money, success, good grades, and each other—and of their collective spiral downward into petty crime, drugs, violence, and eventually murder.

The Breakfast Club (1985) R

The Breakfast Club, John Hughes's watershed teen film, realistically portrays teens in a teen setting. Five disparate teens spend a day together in study hall with inadequate supervision and discover that they are more than their labels. The film portrays teens as teens see themselves, as individuals. As a result of *The Breakfast Club*, subsequent films no longer treated teens as cardboard cutouts. This film changed the way films for teens were made.

The Black Balloon (2008) NR Australia

Sixteen-year-old Thomas Mollison must cope with a new home in the Sydney suburbs, a new school, a potential new girlfriend, a pregnant mother, and living with his 17-year-old autistic brother Charlie.

Bride and Prejudice (2004) PG-13

When Lalita, the oldest of four daughters in an Indian family, meets American millionaire Will Darcy at a family wedding, they, of course, mutually dislike each other. A charming retelling of the original Austen romance with plenty of music and dancing, this film is a Bollywood delight.

The Business of Fancydancing (2002) NR

Sherman Alexie both wrote and directed this story of two friends who grew up on the Spokane Reservation but took two different paths. Seymore is a gay poet who returns to the reservation for a funeral, while Aristotle stayed on the reservation and accomplished nothing. This award-winning film based on Alexie's book, *The Business of Fancydancing*, is a view of an America seldom seen.

The Butterfly Effect (2004) R

An unhappy young man discovers that he can travel in time, but there are awful consequences when he attempts to improve the present by going back and fixing the past.

Childstar (2004) R Canada

An out-of-work independent filmmaker becomes the driver and mentor of a 12-year-old superstar actor. This film shows how both characters come to learn the consequences of fame and of success.

City of Embers (2008) PG

In a post-apocalyptic world, human beings take shelter in the underground city of Ember, created by the ancient Builders. Two hundred years later, the machines are failing and young people Doon and Lina struggle to save their world.

Crazy/Beautiful (2001) PG-13

Privileged wild child Nicole falls for poor, studious Carlos and a rocky and heartfelt romance ensues.

Crossroads (1986) R

Classically trained young guitarist Eugene has a love of vintage blues music. He breaks legendary blues musician Willie Brown, his idol, out of a nursing home to make a scheduled rendezvous with the devil in order to get Willie's soul back.

Cruel Intentions (1999) R

This is the disturbing story of rich, entitled stepsiblings who make a bet on whether the brother can seduce an innocent girl. A modern day if loose interpretation of the French story *Les liaisons dangereuses (Dangerous Liaisons)*, this film depicts teenagers as human monsters.

Dazed and Confused (1993) R

> *Dazed and Confused* is acomedy about the last day of school in a 1970s small town Texas high school. Multiple characters interact during the course of one night as each has adventures of self-discovery. The film is considered another *American Graffiti,* not only because it follows a group of teens throughout the course of just one night, but because many of its young actors went on to become successful. A teen film classic.

Dead Poets Society (1989) PG

> Teacher John Keating strives to inspire his students at a prep school. Roommates Todd and Neil struggle to overcome their families' expectations and become who they want to be.

Deeply (2000) PG Canada

> Grieving teenage violinist Clare and her mother move to an isolated island off the coast of Nova Scotia. When Clare begins reading the manuscript of a local writer, she becomes enthralled with the story of a grief stricken girl named Silly, an island curse, and a passionate love affair. A terrific soundtrack enhances the mythic and evocative elements of *Deeply.*

The Diary of Anne Frank (1959) NR

> In this film version of the classic book, Jewish teen Anne Frank hides with her family from the Nazis in Amsterdam during World War II. There are various other editions of this film, most of them made for television.

Donnie Darko (2001) R

> This film, a teen favorite, is a cult classic about the angst of a teen floating out of his upper middle class Seattle reality and into a dark and terrifying fantasy life.

Double Happiness (1994) PG-13

> In Vancouver, young adult Jade Li is trying to respect her Chinese parents' traditional way of life while falling in love and getting her acting career off the ground. This is a charming film about family love and personal independence.

Dreamland (2006) PG-13

> With almost poetic cinematography and direction, *Dreamland* tells the story of three young people and their families as they sort out their lives and loves in Dreamland, a trailer park located in the middle of nowhere.

Easy Rider (1969) R

> A cultural icon, *Easy Rider* is a journey across the United States by two anti-establishment bikers. Co-written by lead actors Dennis Hopper and Peter Fonda with author Terry Southern, this film relates the good and the bad of the culture and counterculture of the 1960s.

Elephant (2003) R

> Cutting back and forth between the events leading up to and following a Columbine-like shooting, this disturbing film chronicles what should

have been an ordinary day in an ordinary high school. An award winning film by Gus Van Sant, this has the makings of a new classic.

Empire Records (1995) PG-13

When an independent record store is threatened by a takeover from a corporation, the young employees take matters into their own hands. This teen classic has uniformly remarkable performances by a cast that includes Liv Tyler and Renee Zellweger, and is accompanied by a fabulous soundtrack.

Eraserhead (1977) NR Black and white

Director David Lynch's first film is the intriguing and confusing story of Henry, who sports the weird shocked hairdo referenced in the title. Henry spends his time trying to care for a horribly mutated baby, presumably his own by an old girl friend. A cult classic, this is suggested for sophisticated viewers.

Fast Times at Ridgemont High (1982) R

Another watershed teen film, this film is the story of the lives of a group of California high school students, including the unforgettable stoned surfer Spicoli.

Flirting (1991) R Australia

Separate same-sex boarding schools are across the lake from each other, and a stuttering offbeat boy from one falls for a beautiful African girl from the other. This is an extraordinary film that deals with student life as well as intolerance and prejudice.

Four Sheets to the Wind (2007) R

After honoring his suicidal father's last request and burying him in a lake, replacing his body in the coffin with watermelons for the funeral, young Seminole-Cree man Cufe visits his struggling sister in Tulsa and falls for her neighbor.

Fresh (1994) R

This film is a graphic and intense story about a 12-year-old drug runner in Brooklyn. Young Michael ("Fresh") has both promise and a future but simply gets caught up in New York City's endless cycle of violence.

Girl, Interrupted (1999) R

Based on the autobiographical book of the same name, this is the story of Susanna Kaysen and her 18-month stay in a mental hospital after she was diagnosed with borderline personality disorder in the 1960s.

Gorgeous [original title: *Boh lee chun*] (1999) PG-13 Hong Kong/Taiwan

A romantically inclined young girl named Ah Bu finds a message in a bottle and seeks out the writer, who turns out to be gay. Along the way she also meets an older, emotionally closed off banker who discovers that he needs Ah Bu in his life. In a departure from his usual martial arts roles, Jackie Chan plays the banker.

Gregory's Girl (1981) PG United Kingdom

> Gawky but sweet Gregory decides that soccer star beauty Dorothy is for him, but his friends and little sister set things up so that in the end, the right girl gets Gregory.

Good Bye Lenin! (2003) R Germany

> Teen Alex tries to protect his socialist mother from culture shock when she comes out of a nine-month coma during which the Cold War ended and the Berlin Wall was torn down. Slapstick and sweet, this is a funny and touching film that comments on the political mores of Europe at a rapidly changing time. Set in 1990s Germany.

Her Majesty (2001) PG New Zealand

> *Her Majesty* is an award winning film set in 1953 about a town in New Zealand that is about to be visited by Queen Elizabeth, and what 13-year-old Lizzie does to right an injustice done to the family of an elderly Maori.

Homeroom (2002) R

> The aftermath of a Columbine-like high school shooting follows the relationships among three people—a survivor of the massacre, a student who may have some involvement in the incident, and a detective assigned to discover the truth. Although not as polished as *Elephant*, the ending might be more relevant to teens.

How to Deal (2003) PG-13

> Teen heroine Halley decides there is no such thing as true love, and strives to find a place in the world around her. A thoughtful, realistic, and extraordinarily good teen film based on two books by young adult author Sarah Dessen.

In Between Days (2006) NR

> A recent immigrant from Korea, teen Aimie struggles with fitting into a North American city and with her unrequited love for her male best friend who likes Americanized girls.

The Incredibly True Adventures of Two Girls in Love (1995) R

> Randy, a lower class white girl, hates school and lives with her lesbian aunt. Evie is a beautiful, successful African American girl from a well-educated family. The two become friends and then fall in love as their relationship deepens. This is a story about families and what love can really mean.

The Inkwell (1994) R

> The "inkwell" is the African American neighborhood on Martha's Vineyard. This film takes place in 1976 when teen Drew is sent to the island to stay out of trouble and falls for an older woman.

Juno (2007) PG-13

> Sixteen-year-old Juno becomes pregnant after a one night stand with her friend Paulie Bleeker and decides to allow a couple she found in the newspaper to adopt the baby. Juno grows to understand her parents, her baby's prospective adoptive parents, and Paulie, the baby's father.

Kamikaze Girls [original title: *Shimotsuma monogatari*] (2004) NR Japan

Small town teen girls Ichigo and Momoko are nothing alike—Ichigo is a biker chick while Momoko likes to dress as Marie Antoinette—but both strive for an identity, albeit in wildly different ways. As the two girls slowly become friends, they gain acceptance of who they are. Based on Novala Takemoto's novel *Shimotsuma Monogatari*.

Kids Return [original title: *Kizzu ritan*] (1996) NR Japan

Masaru and Shinji are two slackers that pass the time by intimidating their fellow students until they run into someone who trounces them. After they decide to take boxing lessons, their lives change.

Latter Days (2003) R

A 19-year-old Mormon missionary moves to West Hollywood and makes friends with a male neighbor who causes strange feelings of attraction in the young man.

Linda Linda Linda (2005) NR Japan

When a band member is hurt, an all-girls rock band gets a new vocalist and struggles to be ready to perform at their school's cultural days event.

Lucas (1986) PG-13

Lucas is a smart but diminutive kid in high school. He falls for the older Maggie, who has fallen for football player Cappie. This classic teen film respects its characters and their feelings.

Manic (2001) R

Teenager Lyle Jensen is institutionalized after a violent episode at school. This is *One Flew Over the Cuckoo's Nest* for teens.

Mean Girls (2004) PG-13

Home schooled by her parents in Africa, Cady is suddenly thrust into an American high school dominated by a group of catty, popular girls.

A Midsummer Night's Rave (2002) R

What if Shakespeare set his comedy *A Midsummer Night's Dream* in a contemporary Los Angeles rave? This film really manages to stick close to the original story in a delightful retelling of a classic play that appeals to teens.

My Family [also known as *My Family, Mi Familia*] (1995) R

This film relates the story of three generations of a Chicano family in Los Angeles. The story begins with the grandfather, who sneaks into the United States from rural Mexico. Each generation has to deal with what it means to be Latino, urban, and American. A modern classic.

My Summer of Love (2004) R United Kingdom

Mona lives in Yorkshire with her ex-con brother who has found religion. While riding around the Yorkshire countryside, she meets wealthy and socially connected Tamsin. As the summer progresses, the girls find first friendship and then love.

Nana (2005) NR Japan

Nana 2 (2006) NR Japan

> Based on the manga series by Ai Yawaza, two girls named Nana meet on a train, become friends, and share an apartment and new lives in Tokyo.

Napoleon Dynamite (2004) PG-13

> High school student Napoleon Dynamite, who lives in Idaho with his older brother, uncle, and grandmother, is the ultimate geek. But things begin to change when Napoleon becomes the campaign manager for another fish out of water, Pedro, in Pedro's run for class president.

Nearing Grace (2003) R

> In 1970s New Jersey, high school senior Henry struggles with the death of his mother on his own because his family has become too mired in their own messed up lives to help him. Henry drops out of school and spends all his time with two very different girls.

New Waterford Girl (1999) NR Canada

> In this subtle charmer of a film, Moonie Pottie, a 15-year-old girl, struggles to get out of the small town of New Waterford, Nova Scotia and into an art school in New York. She allies with a new streetwise transfer student, a pregnant classmate, and a teacher to attain her dream. With a wonderful and unexpected ending, this film won the Canadian Comedy Award Best Film in 1999.

Noi (2003) PG-13 Iceland

> Noi, a 17-year-old in a small village in Iceland, tries to escape to the outside world and only succeeds in fouling things up.

October Sky (1999) PG

> Based on the book *Rocket Boys* by rocket scientist Homer H. Hickham, Jr. Set in the Sputnik era in the 1950s, this is Hickam's story of growing up in a poor mining community in Appalachia and attempting to build and launch a rocket along with three friends.

Offside (2006) PG Iran

> Six young women, all ardent soccer fans, disguise themselves as men in order to watch the 2006 World Cup game in Azadi Stadium in Iran. When they are caught, they interact with the young soldiers guarding them.

On the Edge (2001) R Ireland

> Actor Cillian Murphy gives a stunning performance as a suicidal teen institutionalized after his father's suicide.

On the Outs (2004) R

> This award winning film tells the story of three girls: a pregnant runaway, a crack addict, and a drug dealer, each of whom has spent time in jail and is trying to survive the mean urban streets.

One Last Thing (2005) R

> Teen Dylan Jameison is terminally ill with cancer and is granted a wish from the Wish Giver's Foundation. He surprises everyone when he asks

for a date with a super model. The film begins as a screwball comedy, but Dylan transforms the lives of everyone he comes in contact with in bittersweet ways.

Ordinary People (1980) R

When one brother drowns in a boating accident and the surviving brother attempts suicide, an upper middle class family begins to disintegrate.

Our Song (2000) R

Our Song is the story of one summer in the lives of three teenage girl-friends from Brooklyn, all of whom are members of a marching band. The three girls face very real issues as they struggle to make it in their neighborhood and beyond.

The Perfect Score (2004) PG-13

Six kids who, for one reason or another, need perfect SAT scores, conspire to steal the answers. This film is a tribute to the teen films of the 1980s. There are consequences for the teens; the ending is not happy, but it is believable.

Pizza (2005) PG-13

Overweight Cara spends the eve of her 18th birthday with Matt, a 30-something pizza delivery guy who takes her on a night full of adventures and revelations.

Platform (2000) NR China

In China during the tumultuous 1980s, four amateur theatre performers in the Fenyang Peasant Culture Group begin their career spouting Maoist rhetoric, but eventually metamorphose into the All Star Rock and Breakdance Electronic Band, flogging Western ideas and influences.

Prom Queen: The Marc Hall Story (2004) NR Made for television Canada

A teenage boy in Ontario, Canada, Marc Hall causes concern and consternation when he brings his boyfriend to the prom at his Catholic high school.

Quinceanera (2006) R

A 15th birthday is a special event in the life of a Hispanic girl named Magdalena. When she becomes pregnant while technically still a virgin, her father kicks her out and she ends up living with an uncle and gay cousin. This film paints a vivid portrait of Magdalena's family and her neighborhood in Los Angeles.

Raising Victor Vargas (2002) R

Victor, along with his brother and sister, are being raised by their crazy Dominican grandmother on the Lower East Side of New York City. When average Victor falls for popular and pretty Judy, this film becomes a sweet, but never cloying, romance and coming-of-age story.

Real Women Have Curves (2002) PG-13

First generation Mexican American Ana has just graduated from Beverly Hills High School, but now lives in East Los Angeles. She works in a dressmaking factory with her mother, who wants more for her daughter. As the title suggests, this is a remarkable film for teenage girls.

Rebel Without a Cause (1955) PG-13

Universally regarded by adults as one of the best teen films ever, this movie follows new kid in town Jim Stark across two days as he meets some new friends and gets involved in the local gang. This film made actor James Dean a teen icon and convinced Hollywood that teen films were worth making. An important film but with limited teen appeal in our experience.

The Red Badge of Courage (1951) NR Black and white
The Red Badge of Courage (1974) NR Made for television

John Huston's 1951 version of Stephen Crane's novel about a young soldier who fears he may prove a coward during the American Civil War is still a masterpiece. The television remake is also good, but suffers in comparison with the first film.

River's Edge (1986) R

One of a group of teens murders his girlfriend, leaves her nude body by the river, and brings the rest of the group to see it. Based loosely on an actual incident, this is a dark and disturbing film.

Rocket Science (2007) R

Plainsboro, New Jersey high school student Hal Hefner is a stutterer from a very dysfunctional family. When Ginny, the girl he falls for, recruits him onto the debate team, Hal's life begins to change.

Run, Lola, Run (1998) R Germany

Lola has 20 minutes to acquire 100,000 Deutsche Marks and get them across town to save the life of her boyfriend Manni, who has lost the money he owes to a drug dealer. A fabulous soundtrack drives this fantasy story of Lola's repeated attempts to make everything come out right. Uniquely existential, time shifting, and briskly paced, this is a classic.

Rushmore (1998) R

Max Fischer is a precocious 15-year-old whose reason for living is Rushmore Academy, the prep school he attends. His life begins to change when he falls for Miss Cross, one of Rushmore's elementary school teachers, and when he befriends his rival for her love, Herman Blume, the eccentric father of two other Rushmore students.

Save the Last Dance (2001) PG-13

Senior Sara blames herself for her mother's death, which occurred while her mother was en route to attend Sara's audition for Juilliard. Now attending a primarily black Chicago high school, Sara ends up dating African American student Derek, and the two help each other try to accomplish their goals.

Saved! (2004) PG-13

Good Christian student Mary sacrifices her virginity to help her boyfriend realize that he isn't gay. It doesn't work, and Mary becomes pregnant, a serious taboo in the Christian high school she attends. The film's fairly predictable happy ending doesn't diminish from a frank story that addresses the notion of faith.

Say Anything... (1989) PG-13

Kick boxer and solid guy Lloyd, played by John Cusack, becomes involved with Diane, a beauty with brains.

The Secret of Roan Inish (1995) PG United States/Ireland

Based on the book *The Secret of Ron Mor Skerry* by Rosalie K. Fry, this John Sayles film is, at heart, a fairy tale about a young girl who learns about her mystical heritage after she and her widowed mother go to live with her grandparents on the west coast of Ireland.

A Separate Peace (2004) R Made for television

Based on the 1959 novel by John Knowles, *A Separate Peace* is the story of the friendship of Gene and Finny at an all boys prep school. A classic and well-crafted film.

Smoke Signals (1998) PG-13

This film, written by Sherman Alexie, is based on his book *The Lone Ranger and Tonto Fistfight in Heaven*. Native Americans Victor and Thomas leave the reservation to go to Phoenix to retrieve the ashes of Victor's father. This heartbreaking and touching story revolves around two sons and two fathers and what they mean to each other.

The Spanish Apartment [original title: *L'auberge espagnole*] (2002) R France

In order to become fluent in Spanish and get the job he wants, a young man decides to spend a year in Barcelona and move into an apartment with a diverse group of young people from many other countries. This film won a Cesar Award, the French equivalent of the Academy Award.

Speak (2004) PG-13 Made for television

Laurie Halse Anderson's book could not have been better adapted for television. A teenage girl is date raped and shuts down both emotionally and physically, becoming a selective mute.

Stand and Deliver (1988) PG

Based on true events, this film tells the story of mathematics teacher Jaime Escalante, who in 1982 convinced his East Los Angeles high school class that they could pass an extremely difficult calculus test. When 18 of them did, the testing agency suspected them of cheating.

Starter for 10 (2006) PG-13 United Kingdom

In 1985 Scotland, a middle-class college student with a penchant for facts finds himself on the University of Bristol's *University Challenge* quiz team and falling for two girls at the same time. An homage to John Hughes's teen films.

Strictly Ballroom (1992) PG Australia

The crazy world of professional ballroom dancing provides the setting for a touching love story between the talented heir to a dancing family legacy and an ordinary girl whom he takes on as his new partner.

Swing Kids (1993) PG-13

In pre WWII Germany, freedoms were usurped while propaganda touted Aryan superiority. Teens who adopted jazz and swing dancing were considered politically disloyal and even criminal, and they were targeted by the *Hitlerjugend* (Hitler Youth). Great music might appeal to many teens.

Thirteen (2003) R

Thirteen-year-old Tracy is a good kid until she befriends popular Evie and the pair begin a downward spiral of self-destructive behavior.

Towelhead [original title: *Nothing is Private*] (2007) R

In this raw portrait of an emotionally lost and abused teen worried about her rampant sexual feelings, 13-year-old Lebanese American Jasira is sent by her mother from Syracuse, New York to live with her father in Houston, Texas, where she encounters racism. For sophisticated viewers.

Train Man [original title: *Densha otoko*] (2005) NR Japan

When loser/geek/gamer Train Man saves a beautiful girl from an attacker on a train, he falls in love and goes to his online community for advice on how to win her. Purportedly based on a true event, this popular story was turned into a book, a comic book, and a television series in Japan.

Trainspotting (1996) R United Kingdom

A heroin addict tries to get clean and sober while still hanging out with his drug-using friends.

Twilight (2008) PG-13

High school student Bella Swan moves to Forks, Washington to live with her father and falls in love with a teen vampire, Edward Cullen. Trouble begins when an out-of-town vampire becomes attracted to her and tries to force Edward out. Based on Stephenie Meyer's best-selling novel for young adults.

The Virgin Suicides (1999) R

Based on the novel by Jeffrey Eugenides, this movie tells the story of the Lisbon family in suburban 1970s Michigan. The five beautiful sisters are the center of the local boys' daydreams, but their strict parents so overwhelm their daughters that the only answer for the girls seems to be death.

A Walk to Remember (2002) PG

Based on the novel by Nicholas Sparks, this is the sweet and real story of a girl who lives strictly by her faith, and who loves a boy so much that he soon realizes he has become a better person for returning her love.

Walkout (2006) NR Made for television

Hispanic students stage a walkout of their East Los Angeles school because of racism, segregation, and unfair educational practices. This film is based on true events of 1968. Edward James Olmos (*Stand and Deliver*) directed this film that premiered on the cable station HBO.

Whale Rider (2002) PG-13 New Zealand

Disqualified because she is both preteen and female, Paikea is passed over as tribal heir to her Maori tribe by her grandfather. But Paikea sets out to prove that women can be as good as men. Set on New Zealand's North Island, this contemporary film is steeped with myth and the old tribal rules.

Zero Day (2007) NR

Focusing on the lives of Cal and Andre during the 11 months leading up to their planned Columbine-like school shooting, this low budget independent film creates a chilling portrait of the prologue to an insanely destructive event. The identities teens find for themselves aren't always healthy ones.

4

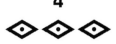

THE APPEAL OF HEROES: SUGGESTED FILMS

It is not uncommon for us to assume that every story has a hero, regardless of the fact that the main characters in films and literature are often *not* heroes but rather antiheros, victims, or bystanders. Nevertheless, this reality does not diminish the appeal to teens of the traditional hero story, in which the main character faces a formidable challenge that he or she struggles valiantly to overcome, often with the aid of a mentor, whose role it is to teach the hero essential skills as well as point out the necessity of drawing upon his or her strength of character. The hero is often accompanied by companions who may be on journeys of their own (think of Sam Gamgee in *The Lord of the Rings*). This formula is especially attractive to young people, particularly because the underdog usually achieves success, but also because the trials faced by the protagonist often parallel the process of growing up.

If you exclude those films listed under sports and competition, most of the films in this chapter are fantasy or science fiction and could be arranged in your collection under those categories. You'll find it hard to categorize many of these films because the films don't distinguish between magic and science. Teens are interested in the power a hero taps into, whatever genre it comes from. The hero is learning to use power, and the appeal for teens is imagining how it would be to have great power.

Comic book heroes of the 1930s and 1940s had young sidekicks because the writers assumed that the readers would identify with the sidekicks. They were wrong; young people identify with heroes and imagine having their powers.

Teens use hero stories as a basis for imagining themselves as heroes in similar situations. Imagining how a hero behaves is a type of creative play that teaches teens how to live as adults. The hero story models attitudes toward adversity, instills idealism, and provides a code of behavior and values that is often very relevant to young people. Sometimes just getting up in the morning to face the world is a heroic act.

SPORTS AND COMPETITION FILMS

When we think of stories about heroes, we are perhaps most likely to think of mythology-based fantasy or science fiction films. However, the category that follows the formula of the hero story most consistently and realistically is that of the sports film. Some films use other sorts of competition, but we will use the term "sports films" as shorthand for films that focus on competition of any kind. Sports films are typically cliché-ridden, but that doesn't diminish their popularity and impact on teens.

The pattern of the sports film is straightforward. The aspiring athlete or team begins as the underdog, facing opponents who are more skilled but also far more arrogant and possibly even corrupted by their success. The underdog is often coached by a mentor figure who, for some reason or another, can no longer play or compete in the game. In many cases, the mentor has lost his appreciation of the game and has become cynical, though he often gains a new respect for the game upon interaction with the hero, who still believes in the game's relevance and importance. Under the mentor's instruction, the hero eventually develops skill for the game while at the same time building inner strength and exhibiting his or her superior character, which is very important, as these are ultimately the factors that will help the hero win the big game. This formula holds true for sports comedies as well, where one of the biggest challenges for the underdog team is their own incompetence.

Although the basic formula of the sports film mirrors that of the traditional hero story, the variations in setting can be enormous. The hero or team of heroes, although usually young, can be male or female, of any race, ethnicity, class, or background. Any sport can be used, and often the contrast between the character and the nature of the sport is an added challenge for the hero. For example, the conflict between working class townies competing in an Italian style bike race against upper class college students in the 1970s Midwest is a twist in the 1979 bike film *Breaking Away*.

The 2002 soccer film *Bend It Like Beckham* follows most sports film conventions, but adds a couple of unique twists that demonstrate what can be done to expand the formula as well as increase its appeal to teens. Jess, the female protagonist of the film, aspires to play soccer as well as her hero, David Beckham. She overcomes adversity to achieve this goal by winning a soccer scholarship with the assistance of her mentor, who helps her develop her skills and her self-reliance.

The twists that make this a distinctive film with particular appeal for teens, especially young female athletes, are triple fold. First, Jess is a teenage female athlete struggling to relate to her conservative parents, who are less interested in her sport than they are in cultivating a demure daughter. Second, there are romantic complications involving her coach that upset her relationship with her best friend on the team. Third, Jess's strict East Indian Sikh heritage comes into direct conflict with the norms of the English society in which she dwells and the goals for which she strives. So, although it falls squarely within the conventions of the typical sports film, *Bend It Like Beckham* adds a search for identity, a glimpse into another culture, and a romantic element. Not only does the heroine need to win in her sport, she must overcome expectations and preconceptions about what and who she should be. The discipline of the sport develops the hero's character so she can face the challenge of creating her own identity.

What to Look for When Selecting

- Be aware of vulgar language and possible crudity, which can be ubiquitous in sports films. Remember, it's always good to preview any film that you're considering adding to your library's collection.
- Look for movies about sports that are popular in your community, but also include movies about unusual sports that might appeal to young people.
- Filmmakers recast the traditional type of character that a sport appeals to, or change the typical community that a sport is played in to give a fresh retelling of the story. Look for films that include characters or communities that might appeal to your teens, whether they're traditional or nontraditional choices.
- Look for films in which young athletes go against the grain and play in nontraditional sports. Stories about the creation of nontraditional sports can be particularly attractive to young people.

- Sports documentaries on which feature films are based are usually good purchases.

Sports and Competition Films

The Basketball Diaries (1995) R

In this film version of Jim Carroll's 1978 cult book *The Basketball Diaries*, Leonardo DiCaprio plays Jim, a poet and basketball star at St. Vitus High School in New York. After Jim spirals down into drugs, he struggles with his addiction, and is ultimately saved by an ex-junkie.

Believe in Me (2006) PG

Based on a true story, this film chronicles the Middleton High, Oklahoma 1964-1965 Lady Cyclones girls' basketball team as they are led to the finals by a male basketball coach forced to take on the job.

Bend It Like Beckham (2002) PG-13

Despite her disapproving Indian parents, English-born Jess collaborates with her friend Juliet to secretly join a girl's soccer team with the intent of getting a scholarship. This film offers a Cinderella-like ending, but with a twist.

Blackballed: the Bobby Dukes Story (2004) NR

Rob Corddry stars in this mockumentary of a paintball champion who attempts a comeback after being banned from the sport.

Blue Crush (2002) PG-13

A surfer heroine attempts a comeback after almost drowning. The scenery and the action are great, and this is one of the few sports films out there with a female protagonist.

Breaking Away (1979) PG

In the era of Lance Armstrong and renewed interest in the sport of cycling, this excellent film no longer seems as dated as it once did. Four local townie kids compete in a team bicycle race with Indiana University students. This is a classic film with broad appeal.

Bustin' Down the Door (2008) NR Documentary

Narrated by actor Edward Norton, this film is about the early days of the sport of surfing in Hawaii and how in the 1970s Australian and South African surfers changed the sport, giving rise to professional surfing.

Chiefs (2002) NR Documentary

Filmmaker/director Daniel Drudge's work follows two years in the career of the Chiefs, a Native American high school basketball team on Wyoming's Wild River Indian Reservation.

Coach Carter (2005) PG-13

Based on the true story of inspirational coach Ken Carter, this film follows the coach's return to his old high school in Richmond, California and his quest to remake the boys' basketball team into a group of accomplished athletes and successful young men.

The Cup [original title: *Phorpa* (1999)] G Bhutan

Shot entirely in a monastery in Bhutan with some of the monastery's personnel, this is the charming story of two young Tibetan refugees who go to great lengths to watch the 1998 World Cup final on television. Sports fans are the same all over the world.

Deck Dogz (2005) NR Australia

Three skateboarding friends struggle to avoid school authorities, their parents, the police, and a criminal element as they attempt to meet their hero, skateboarder Tony Hawk, and compete in his skate competition. Cameo by Tony Hawk.

Dishdogz (2005) PG-13

A young man hired as a dishwasher at an extreme summer camp builds a relationship with the chef, an ex-skateboarding pioneer. The film features cameo performances by real life skateboarders Tony Alva, Ryan Sheckler, and Andy MacDonald.

Edge of America (2003) NR

Shot entirely on the Three Nations Reservation in Salt Lake City, Utah, this made-for-television film is based on the true story of African American teacher Kenny Williams and his tenure as coach of the girls' high school basketball team. This film by Native American filmmaker Chris Eyre premiered at the Sundance Film Festival in 2004.

Eight Below (2006) PG

The real stars of this heroic story are eight abandoned huskies that struggled to survive Antarctic weather for close to six months in 1993 while their human companions tried desperately to find and rescue them.

Final Season (2007) PG

Based on true events, *The Final Season* tells the story of a small town high school baseball team, the Norway High School Tigers, who lose both the coach that led them to 19 consecutive state championships and very probably their school. The girls' volleyball coach takes over the vacant coaching position in an attempt to prove that the baseball team can win again.

Freedom Writers (2007) PG-13

In a stirring film that grapples with racism, hatred, and the realities of urban gang warfare, an inner city teacher encourages her students to express themselves through writing.

Friday Night Lights (2004) PG-13

In the town of Odessa, West Texas, football isn't everything; it's the only thing. Like *Buffy the Vampire Slayer*, this film inspired a popular television series.

Full Ride (2002) PG-13

> High school jock and petty thief Matt Sabo makes it onto the all-star state football team, meets a local girl with a past, and becomes a man. Although the script is sentimental at times, the two main characters are completely believable.

Glory Road (2006) PG

> Based on the true story of Don Haskins, coach of Texas Western University, this film documents the coach's journey to the 1966 NCAA championship title with the first all African American lineup.

Gracie (2007) PG-13

> Based on the true story of the Shue family in New Jersey in 1978, this film follows 15-year-old Gracie's struggle to play competitive soccer in a time when girls' leagues didn't exist.

The Great Debaters (2007) PG-13

> Another film based on actual events, this is the story of small African American Wiley College in 1930s Texas, and how Professor Melvin B. Tolson created one of the best debate teams on record.

The Gridiron Gang (2006) PG-13

> Based on the 1993 television documentary of the same name, this film tells the story of a probation officer at a California juvenile detention facility who starts a football team as a way to reach his wild and violent inmates.

He Got Game (1998) R

> The politics of power and sports come to the forefront in director Spike Lee's story of Jake Shuttlesworth, an inmate who will be released early from prison if he can convince his basketball star son to sign with the governor's alma mater.

The Heart of the Game (2005) PG-13 Documentary

> Ward Serrill's documentary is an extraordinary look at how team players supports each other. Darnellia Russell, star player of Seattle's Roosevelt High School Roughrider girl's basketball team has a baby and then makes a controversial decision to return to play another season. Highly recommended.

Hoop Dreams (1994) PG-13 Documentary

> A fascinating study of the high school careers of two inner city Chicago basketball players as they battle drugs, poverty, and violence to go for the gold of a college scholarship. This film was the winner of the 1993 New York Film Critics Circle and the 1994 National Society of Film Critics for Best Documentary.

Hoosiers (1986) PG

> In this classic period piece, a basketball coach with a checkered past becomes the new coach of an underdog high school basketball team in

a sleepy Indiana farm town and manages to take them to the 1954 state playoffs.

Ice Princess (2005) G

High school science wiz Casey starts off analyzing the physics behind ice skaters' movements for a report and ends up falling in love with the sport, becoming her own test subject, and jeopardizing her plans to go to Harvard.

The Last Game (2002) NR Documentary

This film tells the true story of the 1999 reigning champions of Pennsylvania high school football, the Central Bucks West, and their hard-as-nails coach. A powerful film done on a small budget.

Lords of Dogtown (2005) PG-13

Set in Venice Beach, California (Dogtown) in the 1970s, this is the story of the Z-Boys, three surfers who revolutionize the sport of skateboarding. Features cameos by skateboarders Tony Hawk, Tony Alva, Jay Adams, and others. Based on the documentary "Dogtown and Z-Boys" (2001) PG-13.

Miracle (2004) PG

This unique film covers the entire story of the 1980 U.S. Olympic Gold Medal hockey team, from recruiting the coach and players to the final team and games.

Ping Pong (2002) NR Japan

Based on the popular Japanese graphic novels by Taiyo Matsumoto, this film tells the story of the ups and downs of two ping-pong players on a school team. The action during the games is astounding.

Ping Pong Playa (2007) PG-13

Chinese-American slacker Christopher "C-dub" Wang is all about basketball, while his family is all about ping pong. When his parents are injured, he has to run the family store and teach ping pong at the community center.

Pride (2007) PG

A coach at an inner city recreation center in 1970s Philadelphia leads his swimmers to greatness while fighting racism. Loosely based on a true story.

Remember the Titans (2000) PG

Based on true events, this film documents the story of the court-ordered integration of three high schools in Alexandra, Virginia in 1971. White head coach Bill Yoast is asked to step down in favor of African American coach Herman Boone, and the two of them must overcome many obstacles to create a winning team.

Rocks with Wings (2002) NR Documentary

Filmmaker Rick Derby's look at African American athlete-turned-teacher Jerry Richardson as he first takes on the job as coach of the 1987 girls' high school basketball team in the Navajo community of Shiprock, New Mexico.

The Rookie (2002) G

If Coach Jim Morris's losing high school team wins the district championship, its players want Jim to try out for a major league organization. Based on the real-life story of Jim Morris, this is a great family film about the great American pastime.

Step into Liquid (2003) PG Documentary

Documentary filmmaker Dana Brown does for modern day surfing what his father, documentary filmmaker Bruce Brown, did in the classic surfing documentary *The Endless Summer* (1966) PG.

Stick It (2006) PG-13

Having walked away from the U.S. Women's Olympic gymnastics team, a young and troubled gymnast makes a court-ordered comeback.

Varsity Blues (1999) R

This MTV-produced film preceded *Friday Night Lights* and features Texas, football, winning, coaches, and underdogs. The West Canaan Coyotes football team is playing for their 23rd division title when an incident forces the second string coach to the fore.

Wondrous Oblivion (2003) PG United Kingdom

Eleven-year-old David Wiseman's immigrant Jewish family were the outsiders in their London neighborhood until a Jamaican family moves in next door and, to David's delight, puts up a cricket pitch in the backyard. This movie is about prejudice, racism, and how the love of a sport can level the playing fields between people.

The Year of the Bull (2003) NR Documentary

What *Hoop Dreams* does for basketball, *The Year of the Bull* does for football. This is the story of the senior year of All American high school football player, Taurean Charles, and his struggle to get into college.

The Year of the Yao (2004) PG Documentary

The Year of the Yao is the amazing but true story of the NBA's first Chinese player, 22-year-old Yao Ming, on and off the court.

"LIVE ACTION HEROES PLUS" FILMS

Heroes in adult action adventure films don't need to have superpowers or use magic, but films aimed at teens that fall into the action adventure genre require that their heroes have supernatural or super scientific powers, skills, and gadgets. The divide between fantasy, science fiction, and action adventure has blurred into a new category that's really too broad to be called a genre.

Advances in special effects technology mean that elements of storytelling that once could appear only in comics and graphic novels can now appear in live action films. Stories from mythology, science fiction, fantasy, comic books, and martial arts are compressing into a new category of film that's still waiting for a name, such as "Graphical Storytelling" or "Augmented Live Action. Coming up with a term for this type of film is difficult, but "Live Action Heroes Plus" captures the idea that the characters, whether animated or live-action, and their stories are no longer limited by reality. The films that fall into this group share a great appeal for teens because they tap into teens' desire for great powers and wish fulfillment.

Adherence to the traditional hero storyline is looser in these films because plot lines and conventions from superhero comics, martial arts films, and science fiction are brought into the mix. The hero story might work initially, as a character becomes a Superman-type hero or a martial arts master, but it is harder to maintain when the story isn't nicely wrapped up and threatens to become soap opera. The hero story is a closed story and no one questions that the hero lives happily ever after.

The *Spider-Man* films exemplify the evolution of the hero in the context of this new class of films. Peter Parker, the protagonist, begins the trilogy as an ordinary teen who gets picked on for being the photographer for the student yearbook. He lives with his Aunt May and Uncle Ben, adoptive parents who have tried to raise Peter to become a good man. When a radioactive spider bites him, Peter develops superhuman abilities and starts a process of learning about his new powers through trial and error—at which point he is forced to face the problem of what to do with those powers. His Uncle Ben, acting as both parent and mentor, advises him that "with great power comes great responsibility." After a criminal that Peter had both the ability and opportunity to stop kills Uncle Ben, Peter realizes that his powers must be used for good. In the sequels, Peter as Spider-Man faces problems of despair, ego, and ennui, while at the same time Peter as an everyday young person faces problems with such ordinary things as relationships and jobs.

Teens know that they have extraordinary talents to offer the world, but struggle to know what to do with them and how to do what's best. They appreciate superhero films, both as avenues for escape and as metaphors for their lives.

What to Look for When Selecting

- Remember that established heroes such as the X-Men, Superman, and Batman circulate even when the reviews are mediocre.
- Look for films based on graphic novels by well-known writers or artists.

- Search out films produced or directed by noted professionals from the fields of comic books and graphic novels.

"Live Action Heroes Plus" Films

30 Days of Night (2007) R

When the month-long winter night comes to an isolated Alaskan town, a gang of vampires attack while the town's sheriff and his wife struggle to keep the remaining humans alive. Based on the graphic novels of Ben Templeton and Steve Niles.

300 (2006) R

A visually stunning version of Frank Miller's epic graphic novel of the same name, this is the story of the 300 Spartans at the battle of Thermopylae. This film was spoofed in the film *Meet the Spartans* (2008) PG-13.

Aeon Flux (2005) PG-13

Based on an animated MTV series about a futuristic totalitarian society, this film takes place in 2415, roughly 400 years after a pandemic has killed off virtually the entire population of the planet. Aeon Flux, the female protagonist, is a rebel assassin who, when sent on a mission to destroy a government leader, uncovers a host of sinister secrets about how her society sustains itself.

Batman Begins (2005) PG-13
The Dark Knight (2008) PG-13
Batman Franchise (1989 to 1997) PG-13

Batman Begins depicts the early life of Bruce Wayne and is a prequel to the *Batman* film franchise. Christian Bale reprises his *Batman Begins* role in *The Dark Knight*.

Blade (1998) R
Blade II (2002) R
Blade: Trinity (2004) R

Marvel Comics character Blade was born to a woman who was bitten by a vampire while she was pregnant with him. As a result, Blade became half human and half vampire, growing up to harbor a bitter hatred of vampires. With impressive special effects and a striking style, these are exciting films.

Blade Runner (1982) R

Based on Philip K. Dick's science fiction classic, *Do Androids Dream of Electric Sheep?*, Ridley Scott's film creates a dark future where the police hunt down rogue androids. Later director's cut editions are considered better versions than the original.

Catwoman (2004) PG-13

Although Catwoman has been a prime role for many actresses over the years, Halle Berry's version is disappointing. Never mind—the fans won't care about that.

The Clash of the Titans (1981) PG

> A Ray Harryhausen stop motion special effects extravaganza details the exploits of Perseus and how he is both aided and impeded by the Greek gods.

The Crow (1994) R

> The original film, starring Brandon Lee, son of martial artist Bruce Lee, set the standard for the *film noir* comic book film. Brandon Lee died during the film's production, however, and the sequels never quite measured up to the original.

Daredevil (2003) PG-13

> Blind attorney Matt Murdock fights crime by day as a lawyer in Hell's Kitchen and by night as Daredevil, a masked avenger with a highly acute radar sense. Daredevil's love interest is another superhero, Elektra Natchios. Based on an original work by Frank Miller and Marvel Comics.

Doom (2005) R

> This film is based on the legendary computer game "Doom" and stars wrestler Dwayne "The Rock" Johnson.

Elektra (2005) PG-13

> In another Frank Miller comic come to life, and a spinoff of the *Daredevil* film, super-heroine Elektra has been hired by a mysterious organization called The Hand to kill a father and his young daughter. When Elektra gets to know the pair, she switches sides to protect them.

Enter the Dragon (1973) R Hong Kong/United States

> Shaolin monk and secret agent Bruce Lee goes undercover in this seminal martial arts film. Lee died at age 32 soon after the film was released.

Fantastic Four (2005) PG-13
Fantastic Four: Rise of the Silver Surfer (2007) PG

> These films are mediocre but enjoyable treatments of the adventures of Marvel Comics popular superhero troupe, The Fantastic Four.

Final Fantasy: The Spirits Within (2001) PG-13

> Very loosely based on the *Final Fantasy* videogame franchise, this film is what great computer generated animation should look like.

A Fistful of Dollars (1964) R Italy
For a Few Dollars More (1965) Italy
The Good, The Bad and The Ugly (1966) R Italy

> Perhaps the most famous of spaghetti Westerns, Sergio Leone's Dollars Trilogy stars Clint Eastwood as the Man With No Name, a larger than life, almost mythic character. In the first film, the Man helps the residents of a Mexican village caught between two rival gangs. In the second, the Man and another bounty hunter are out to capture the notorious El Indio. The last film is the story of three men after a cache of gold.

Forbidden Kingdom [Original title: Gong fu zhi wang] (2008) United States/China
PG-13

An American teen finds the legendary Chinese weapon of the Monkey King in a pawnshop and is transported back to Ancient China. There, he and his companions must fight to free the imprisoned Monkey King.

Ghost Dog: the Way of the Samurai (1999) R

Forest Whitaker plays Ghost Dog, an African American hitman who follows the Code of the Samurai. When a low level mobster, Louie, from Jersey City, saves his life, Ghost Dog becomes obligated to Louie as his master. When a mob boss orders Louie to kill the hitman, Ghost Dog finds himself having to protect the man who is out to kill him.

Ghost World (2001) R

This film is a live action version of the 1998 graphic novel of the same name by Daniel Clowes. This was the first film to receive an Oscar nomination for Best Adapted Screenplay based on a Graphic Novel or Comic Book.

Ghost Rider (2007) PG-13

A minor character from Marvel Comics, stunt motorcyclist Johnny Blaze sells his soul to save his terminally ill father.

Hellboy (2004) PG-13
Hellboy II: the Golden Army (2008) PG-13
Hellboy: Sword of Storms (2006) NR Animated

Ron Perlman brings Hellboy to life in this film version of Mike Mignola's inimitable hero. The special effects are great, and *Hellboy I* and *II* never take themselves too seriously. *Hellboy: Sword of Storms* is the first of several animated feature-length films with Ron Perlman voicing the lead role.

Hero [Original title: Ying xoing] (2002) PG-13 China

A nameless warrior travels to the imperial court to tell the emperor the story of how he bested the emperor's enemies in this visually spectacular film.

House of Flying Daggers (2004) PG-13 China

Visually stunning, majestic, and epic, this martial arts film is at its heart a love story. Hollywood has never produced a film like this.

Hulk (2003) PG-13

This is a critically disappointing Hollywood live action version of the Marvel Comics antihero. It proved popular because fans hadn't seen the Hulk since the 1970s television show. This is a secondary choice.

The Incredible Hulk (2008) PG-13

This new version of the Hulk has extraordinary special effects and is preferable to the 2003 version.

Judge Dredd (1995) R

In a dystopian future, Street Judges roam the mean streets and dispense justice on the spot. One of these judges, the eponymous Judge Dredd, is wrongfully convicted of a crime while the real murderer goes free.

Lara Croft, Tomb Raider (2001) PG-13
Lara Croft, The Cradle of Life (2003) PG-13

The aristocratic, sexy, and kick-butt heroine Lara Croft jumps from the videogame franchise to the big screen in these two solid action flicks.

The League of Extraordinary Gentlemen (2003) PG-13

The graphic novels of the same name are much better than this Hollywood treatment of them. The film is little more than special effects gone overboard and has none of the wit or plot line of the original novels. This film is a secondary choice for selection, but it might lead your teens to the sources.

Mad Max (1979) R Australia
Mad Max 2: the Road Warrior (1981) R Australia
Mad Max Beyond Thunderdome (1985) PG-13 Australia/United States

Set in a dystopic future Australia where gasoline has become more valuable than gold and biker gangs are taking over, police officer Max Rockatansky, played by Mel Gibson, sets out to avenge his wife and child after they are killed by gang leader Toecutter. In the sequels, Max continues to protect the innocent and the weak.

The Magnificent Seven (1960) NR

Based on Japanese film director Akira Kurosawa's *Seven Samurai*, a Mexican town that is being terrorized by bandits hires gunmen to come and protect the town. The gunmen help the villagers defeat their enemies themselves. Although the characters are realistic, the overall work has a mythic quality that sets it apart from typical Westerns.

The Matrix (1999) R
The Matrix Revisited (2001) NR Documentary
The Matrix Reloaded (2003) R
The Matrix Revolutions (2003) R
The Animatrix (2003) PG-13 Animated

The first installment of this franchise is the film that all cult films of the past 10 years have tried to live up to. Thomas Anderson's hacker persona Neo meets the mysterious Morpheus who proves to him that his life is a lie. Neo joins Morpheus to save the world from the machines that have enslaved the human race.

Men in Black (1997) PG-13
Men in Black II (2002) PG-13

Special agents K and J keep Earth's underground alien residents in line and save the planet from total destruction. These films are hip, funny, and have great special effects.

Once Upon A Time in the West (1968) PG-13 Italy/United States

Another Sergio Leone Western, this time with American actors Henry Ford and Charles Bronson, this is, perhaps, the iconic Western film. A young woman moves to a remote Utah town to join her new husband and family only to discover that they have all been killed. When she becomes the target of an outlaw in the pay of the railroad, two men come to her aid: a harmonica-playing stranger and a gunslinger on the run from the law. This film doesn't have the mythic quality of Leone's spaghetti Westerns filmed in Italy, but if your teens enjoy those films, they might enjoy this despite it being a Western with conventional characters.

Punisher (2004) R

Based on the Marvel Comics hero, this film tells the story of special agent Frank Castle and his evolution into the avenging Punisher after the death of his wife and child.

Resident Evil (2002) R
Resident Evil: Apocalypse (2004) R
Resident Evil: Extinction (2007) R

Based on the *Resident Evil* videogame franchise, these films and their soundtracks appeal to both gamers and horror/science fiction fans.

The Rocky Horror Picture Show (1975) R

A box office flop when it opened, this film has become a cult classic, necessary for cultural literacy. It tells the story of what can happen to two white middle class young adults when they meet an alien "sweet transvestite from Transsexual, Transylvania." This film is not based on a comic book, but the out there cinematography and costumes make it a good example of graphical storytelling.

Road to Perdition (2002) R

A hit man and his son go on the run during the Depression. This film was based on a DC graphic novel.

Sin City (2005) R

Exquisitely stylized to look exactly like the Frank Miller graphic novels, this is a brilliant piece of filmmaking. Be warned that it is excessively violent and for the sophisticated viewer only.

Spider-Man (2002) PG-13
Spider-Man 2 (2004) PG-13
Spider-Man 3 (2007) PG-13

This big-budget version of Peter Parker's transformation into Spider-Man is a great blend of CGI (computer generated imagery) and live action. The villains are memorable, and so is Tobey Maguire's portrayal of Spidey.

The Spirit (2008) PG-13

This adaptation of Will Eisner's 1940s comic book, in which former cop Denny Colt transformed into super crime fighter The Spirit, has highly stylized animation and spoofs comics and American popular culture following World War II.

Star Trek (2009) PG-13

Director J.J. Abrams's reinvention of the classic franchise has created a new generation of fans and should spark a new interest in the older Star Trek movies for science fiction fans of all ages.

Star Wars Franchise
Star Wars: Episode IV: A New Hope (1977) PG
Star Wars: Episode V: The Empire Strikes Back (1980) PG
Star Wars: Episode VI: Return of the Jedi (1983) PG
Star Wars: Episode I: The Phantom Menace (1999) PG
Star Wars: Episode II: Attack of the Clones (2002) PG
Star Wars: Episode III: Revenge of the Sith (2005) PG-13
Star Wars: The Clone Wars (2008) PG Animated feature length.

George Lucas created this modern mythos that has spawned millions of fans. These films follow the epic journey of two pairs of young people: Anakin and Padme, and their children, Luke and Leia.

Stay Alive (2006) PG-13

Friends playing the videogame *Stay Alive* begin dying the same way their avatars do online.

Superman Franchise (1978 to 1987)
Superman Returns (2006) PG-13

Superman is reinvented for the big screen in every generation. Nearly 20 years after the Christopher Reeves versions of the 1970s and '80s, a subdued and sad Superman is back in *Superman Returns.*

Teen Titans: Trouble in Tokyo (2007) NR

In this feature-length version of the animated series, the Titans, sidekicks of the Justice League, battle the evil Saico Tek. A better than average video.

TMNT (2007) PG

TMNT is a total CGI (computer-generated imagery) version of the *Teenage Mutant Ninja Turtles* that has significant nostalgia value for the generation that grew up with the Turtles on Saturday-morning television.

V for Vendetta (2005) R

In 2020 Great Britain, vigilante V wears a Guy Fawkes mask as he battles the totalitarian government in this stylish but otherwise weak adaptation of the Alan Moore graphic novel.

The Watchmen (2009) R

In an alternative 1985 where Richard Nixon is still president, America's superheroes have been sidelined for a decade by the government until one of the retired superheroes is murdered. Allan Moore and Dave Gibbon's classic graphic novel gets a star turn in this excellent movie.

X-Men (2000) PG-13
X2 (2003) PG-13
X-Men: The Last Stand (2006) PG-13
Numerous Animated X-Men films

> Hollywood did a great job of bringing this historic Marvel comic book series to the big screen. Teens identify with these characters, who feel out of sync with the rest of the world, but who follow the hero's journey to completeness as they learn to work together and use their talents.

X-Men Origins: Wolverine (2009) PG-13

> In 1840s British North America, half-brothers Jimmy Logan and Victor Creed discover they are mutants since Victor sports fangs and Logan has claws. This origin story reveals the reason for Logan's anger and why he undergoes the surgery that makes him Wolverine.

ANIME AND OTHER ANIMATED FILMS

Anime, a tradition of animated films developed in Japan, has completely revolutionized modern day teen films, both animated and live action. Anime has a distinctive style, but more significantly, it makes use of cinematographic techniques for storytelling. Traditional animation is made as though from a fixed-point camera filming a stage play. The point of view in anime is much more like that of film, moving and showing views of the action from all directions. Anime takes advantage of all the techniques of filmmaking to tell stories. Animated films are no longer just for children anymore.

In the 1960s and 1970s, the American film industry overwhelmed the Japanese film industry in all areas except animated films. The energy and vision of the Japanese film industry concentrated on animated films made for all ages and interests.

Today, most anime films imported to the United States were produced for Japanese junior and young adult viewers. Therefore, they generally feature the hero storyline very prominently and appropriately. A young boy, girl, or group of boys and/or girls is given a challenge to overcome, and oftentimes extraordinary powers with which to overcome it. The strength that comes from character, which allows the hero to overcome adversity, is more explicitly discussed in these films than in American films. The characters also face their shortcomings directly, which is a useful example for teens in that it shows that flaws don't necessarily represent failures of character, but sometimes just come from lack of experience or simple lapses in judgment.

Ever since anime's revolution in the 1960s, the storytelling in Japanese animation has been more sophisticated than that in American animation.

Characters are more fully fleshed out, well rounded, and do not always enjoy a traditional Disney-style happy ending. Additionally, anime films tell interesting stories, deal with issues that resonate with teens, and employ vigorous use of music and action. In recent years, producers of American animated films have learned a great deal from Japanese films about how to appeal to teens, including using strong storylines and the aforementioned strong heroic characters, both male and female

"Anime" is the term for all Japanese animated films, and, as such, includes a very broad category of films aimed at many audiences. The anime that has been imported for American audiences is intended for children to teens, but it is still a very broad assortment of works. Your teen patrons will likely have discovered their favorite genres within anime and educated themselves about them. Find out what they want to develop the collection you need to serve your local population.

One of the most influential anime creators working now is Hayao Miyazaki, who is the guiding vision behind Studio Ghibli. His works are among the few that can be said to be required for any film collection. Any film that Miyazaki is connected with can be recommended for family viewing, though it must be said that some of the darker moments in his films might be too much for younger children. Evidence of the impact that anime in general, and Studio Ghibli more specifically, has had on American films in recent years is the fact that The Walt Disney Company recently purchased the right to distribute many of the studio's films in the United States. Miyazaki films are especially appropriate for library film programs because the attention to detail and sheer beauty of the animation lend themselves well to larger screens.

Miyazaki usually chooses plots in which the hero is a girl or young woman who has to find inner strength to overcome adversity. For example, the film *Howl's Moving Castle* (2005), based on Diana Wynne Jones' book of the same name, features a young woman named Sophie Hatter. Sophie is cursed by the evil Witch of the Waste and turned into an elderly woman. Her quest is to break the spell, but along the way, she finds out about herself and her strengths while making a difference in other peoples' lives. As a result of her kindness and willingness to pitch in where she is needed, she redeems others and helps Howl, an attractive young wizard under an enchantment, regain his humanity.

Howl's Moving Castle definitely falls into the category of the hero's tale, but unlike Western hero films, the entire cast of characters is well developed. It is also very important to notice that the evil characters aren't depicted as all evil, but instead contain a more realistic mixture of good and bad. The Witch of the Waste, who begins the story by cursing Sophie, becomes a respected member of the castle's household in the end. The witch actually helps Sophie cure Howl and herself of their enchantments. Howl's former mentor views him as an unstable and selfish character and marks him for destruction. Sophie redeems his character, and his mentor concedes that she was wrong. In short, the good characters have their flaws and the bad characters have their good points.

The first thing that a new anime viewer will likely notice about anime films is that the characters all seem to be Caucasian. This nuance might give the impression that the films were tailored for American and European audiences, but this is not the case. Rather, the characters look the way they do because it is important that their eyes be unusually large and expressive, even for people of Caucasian background, in order to better express emotion. Hair color often works as an indicator of character as well. For example, Sophie, the main character of *Howl's Moving Castle*, begins the film with dark brown hair and eyes, which signal that she is a level headed person. Howl, the magician she falls in love with, changes his hair color repeatedly until the end when his hair reverts to his childhood color of black. This signals to us that he is an unstable person who needs Sophie's love to ground him.

Many people tend to think of Japan as a place where high technology and tradition coexist but don't overlap, except in picturesque photos. Anime blends magic and technology seamlessly allowing a pseudo-Victorian society to have flying machines and clockwork castles that walk cross-country. This is typical of a subgenre of anime films that falls in the category of "steampunk," a type of science fiction that combines advanced technology and pseudo-historical, romantic settings One of anime's appeals is the remarkable amount of imagination it puts into the settings, while maintaining a deeply human touch.

What to Look for When Selecting

- Purchase anything by Osamu Tezuka, Hayao Miyazaki, or Studio Ghibli for your library, although some of their films might be more appropriate for a junior collection.
- Talk to your teen patrons, and you will undoubtedly find anime fans. Ask their advice on what to add, and you will never lack for suggestions.
- Check what anime is being shown on the Disney Channel, the Action Channel, and Cartoon Network.

- At the current time, any anime title, including similar productions from Korea, is likely to circulate, but check for ratings when available and make sure to preview if none are available.

- A new approach to animation is motion comics, which takes artwork from comic books and graphic novels, animates images from existing panel art, and enhances it with voice actors and a music soundtrack. *Watchmen: The Complete Motion Comic* came out in 2009 and motion comics starring Batman are scheduled for release. If it catches on, a huge number of popular comic book storylines from publishers like DC and Marvel are likely to become motion comics.

Anime and Other Animated Films

Feature length film titles are listed below; recommended anime series or boxed sets appear at the end of this list.

5 Centimeters Per Second [original title: *Byosoku 5 Senchimetoru*] (2007) PG Made for television Japan

Writer/director Makoto Shinkai's beautifully animated work is a collection of three short stories all having to do with time. The title refers to the rate of speed at which cherry blossoms fall from a tree.

Akira (1988) R Japan

This classic anime masterpiece of a corrupt, dystopian future is violent and therefore most appropriate for older teens.

Allegro Non Troppo (1977) NR Italy

Italian animator Bruno Bozetto's tribute to *Fantasia* (1940), this video is a series of shorts set to music by Dvorak, Debussy, Ravel, and Stravinsky. Animation fans will find it a classic.

Animatrix (2003) PG-13

Animatrix, nine short subjects from an international team of animation creators, is simply a showstopper. "The Second Renaissance" (parts 1 & 2) fills in some of the backstory of the film *The Matrix*. Each of the creators used cutting edge animation, computer generated imagery, and live action techniques to produce an amazing DVD.

Aqua Teen Hunger Force Colon [sic] Movie Film For Theaters (2007) R

This is an animated film version of the popular animated television show from the Adult Swim late night block on the Cartoon Network.

Beauty and the Beast (1991) G

The Disney version of the fairy tale of the same name, this is a popular love story especially enjoyed by young women. For teen and children's collections.

Bleach the Movie: Memories of Nobody [original title: *Gekijouban Bleach*] (2006) NR
   Japan

   A mystery develops for Ichigo and Rukia with the sudden appearance
   of unidentified creatures called Blanks and a Soul Reaper, who makes
   the Blanks disappear. Based on the popular anime and manga series, this
   film will prove popular.

Blood: the Last Vampire (2000) NR Japan

   An interestingly animated story about vampires on a 1966 U.S. airbase.

Broken Saints (2001) NR

   Not actually a film, this boxed set is a video experience consisting of
   numerous episodes of varying lengths and diverse animation techniques.
   This Internet project is the creation of Brooke Burgess, Andrew West, and
   Ian Kirby and has been running online for years. Four strangers, an Iraqi
   soldier, a computer programmer, a Shinto monk, and an orphan girl
   raised on Fiji all experience an apocalyptic vision of the end of the world
   and come together to save it.

The Chronicles of Riddick: Dark Fury (2004) NR

   Unique animation of this 30-minute long video features Vin Diesel doing
   the voice for his Riddick character from the film *Pitch Black*. Violent and
   gory, it's a film Riddick fans will love. Look for some of the other animated films based on the Chronicles of Riddick if this proves of interest
   to your teen patrons.

The Corpse Bride (2005) PG

   The Corpse Bride is a Tim Burton "animation noir" like his 1993 *Nightmare
   Before Christmas*. Groom Victor van Dort is to marry, but winds up in the
   Land of the Dead, saddled with the wrong bride.

Cowboy Bebop: Knockin' on Heaven's Door [original title: *Kauboi bibappu: Tengoku no
   tobira*] (2001) R Japan

   Cowboy Bebop: Knockin' on Heaven's Door is series creator Shinichiro
   Watanabe's film version of the adventures of bounty hunters Spike
   Spiegel, Jet Black, and Faye Valentine. They travel aboard the spaceship
   Bebop tracking nasty criminal Vincent Volaju in 2071 with the help of kid
   computer expert, Edward, and wonder dog Einstein.

Dark Crystal (1982) PG

   Jim Henson's mythic tale of good and evil is a modern classic. In order
   to defeat the evil Skeksis, Gelflings Jen and Kira must restore the missing
   shard to the Dark Crystal.

Enchanted (2007) PG

   The film begins in an animated Disney-style world before the fairytale
   princess is transported to all-too-real New York City. This delightful
   romance features plenty of music.

Fantasia 2000 (1999) G

An entertaining homage to the original *Fantasia* (1940), and years in the making, this film complements rather than replaces its predecessor. *Fantasia 2000* clearly takes some ideas from the original: Stravinsky's "The Rite of Spring" is like *Fantasia*'s "Night on Bald Mountain/Ave Maria" sequence, but it's a great sequel.

Fantastic Planet [original title: *La Planete Sauvage*] (1973) PG France

Humanoid Oms are slaves to the giant Draags, until an Om starts a revolution to gain their freedom.

Flatland (2007) NR

An animated version of the 1884 mathematical fantasy book by Edwin Abbott, this is an intriguing attempt to portray multi-dimensional worlds.

Final Fantasy VII: Advent Children (2005) PG-13

A follow up to the videogame *Final Fantasy VII*, this is what great computer generated animation should look like. After an alien invasion, a small force of the remaining humans fight to regain their world.

Ghost in the Shell [original title: *Kokaku kidotai*] (1995) NR Japan

In the year 2929, a female cyborg agent must apprehend an intelligent computer program, the Puppet Master, before it becomes completely sentient.

Grave of the Fireflies [original title: *Hotaru no haka*] (1988) NR Japan

Teen Seita and his four-year-old sister survive the bombing of their city during World War II only to struggle to survive the aftermath.

Howl's Moving Castle [original title: *Haura no ugoku shiro*] (2004) PG Japan

Based on the fantasy novel by Diana Wynne Jones, this is another Hayao Miyazaki triumph. It tells the story of hat maker Sophie, who runs afoul of a witch and joins the strangest household ever to travel the countryside, falling in love with its cursed owner, Howl.

Kaena: The Prophecy [original title: *Kaena: La Prophetie*] (2003) PG-13 France, Canada, United States

In this science fiction/fantasy film, the young and rebellious teen Kaena fights to save her people and their world. However, this computer generated animation feature by a French/American team was originally 3D, and in 2D some of the effects are just weird.

The Little Mermaid (1989) G

Another Disney animated film, like *Beauty and the Beast*, this popular love story is appropriate for a teen collection as well as a children's collection. *The Little Mermaid: Ariel's Beginning* is a prequel that was released in 2008, and may be of interest as well.

Metropolis [original title: *Metoroporisu*] (2001) PG-13 Japan

> *Metropolis* is an excellent anime retelling by Osamu Tezuka of Fritz Lang's classic science fiction story by the same name. In a gorgeous city of the future, life is paradise for the wealthy, who are protected from seeing the hell life is for the poor. A privileged boy befriends a little girl who turns out to be a robot who can destroy the city.

Nausicaa of the Valley of the Wind [original title: *Kaze no tani no Naushika*] (1984) PG Japan

> *Nausicaa of the Valley of the Wind* is another Hayao Miyazaki epic about survival in a post-apocalyptic world. Princess Nausicaa strives to keep her people safe in the midst of a poisonous jungle.

The Nightmare Before Christmas (1993) PG

> Tim Burton's first animated film is a watershed effort, affecting the art of animation in later films and shorts. This film has been a cult classic from its first release.

Persepolis (2007) PG-13 France

> *Persepolis* is a unique black and white animated feature film directed by Marjane Satrapi, based on her graphic novels about a young girl's coming of age in Iran and Europe.

Pixar Short Films Collection Volume 1 (2007) G

> This collection of shorts showcasing the early days of Pixar Studios is a revealing study in the history of computer-generated animation.

Pokemon: The Movie (2000) G Japan

> Pokemon's trainer Ash must return three glass balls to their rightful place in order to save the planet. There are other Pokemon films, but this anime, directed by Kunihiko Yuyama, has been especially popular among teen males.

Princess Mononoke [original title: *Mononoke-hime*] (1997) PG-13 Japan

> Veteran filmmaker Hayao Miyazaki wrote the screenplay for the original film, and Neil Gaiman wrote the English version. Mononoke is the myth-like story of man versus nature and evil versus good as well as a tender love story between Ashitaka, who tries to bring peace to the world, and San, who fights for the animals and the forest.

Renaissance (2006) R France

> Director Christian Volckman uses a live action, motion capture computer animation technique that creates a stark black and white *film noir* effect. Police officer Karas sets out to find a missing geneticist. Originally in French, a dubbed English language version is also available. Set in Paris in 2054.

A Scanner Darkly (2006) R

> Based on the 1977 Phillip K. Dick novel of the same name, an undercover narcotics policeman becomes an addict himself. Director Richard

Linklater's rotoscoping animation technique gives this film just the right surreal drug-like atmosphere.

The Simpsons Movie (2007) PG-13

You don't need to be a fan of the television show to appreciate this movie. The plot doesn't break new ground, but the animation is especially well done.

South Park: Bigger, Longer, & Uncut (1999) R

If you like the television show, you'll like this. "Blame Canada" was nominated for an Oscar as Best Music/Original Song.

Spirited Away [original title: *Sen to Chihiro no kamikakushi*] (2002) PG

When 10-year-old Sen and her parents stumble upon a deserted theme park, the parents mysteriously transform into pigs. Renamed Chihiro, Sen follows them to a mad bathhouse, where she meets Haku, who helps her on a wild quest to find and restore her parents. Another Miyazaki masterpiece.

Star Wars: The Clone Wars (2008) PG Animated

George Lucas creates an animated version of his beloved franchise. Not to be confused with *Star Wars: The Clone Wars* (2003), the animated television series that bridged the plot gap between *Star Wars: Episode II: Attack of the Clones* and *Star Wars: Episode III: Revenge of the Sith*.

Steamboy [original title: *Suchimuboi*] (2004) PG-13 Japan

A boy receives a powerful "steam ball" and must fight the evil O'Hara Foundation. This is a classic example of "steampunk," a science fiction subgenre set in an alternate Victorian world where advanced technology is based on steam power. Set in Victorian England.

Superman: Doomsday (2007) PG-13 Animated

A great variation on the traditional superhero story, this is the story of what happens after Superman's death. Based largely on the "Death of Superman" story arc from the DC comics, Superman battles the living weapon Doomsday, a creature that defeats and kills him. Heroes appear to replace him, one of whom seems to be Superman reborn.

Tales of Earthsea [original title: *Gedo Senki*] (2006) NR Japan

Tales of Earthsea is Studio Ghibli's version of the Ursula K. Le Guin fantasy trilogy.

Titan AE (2000) PG

One thousand years in the future, Cale, son of the scientist that created the Titan Project, must save the planet Earth from imminent destruction. From Twentieth Century Fox, directors Don Bluth (*Anastasia*) and Gary Goldman combine computer generated and traditional animation to create a visual masterpiece.

Treasure Planet (2002) PG

> *Treasure Planet* is the Disney studio's space opera version of Robert Louis Stevenson's *Treasure Island*.

Vampire Hunter D [original title: *Banpaia hanta D*] (1985) NR Japan

> Half vampire and half human, D fights monsters in a violent and dark world. For sophisticated viewers due to violence.

Waking Life (2001) R

> Digitally shot with human beings, the film was distributed among 30 artists who transformed their footage through interpolated rotoscoping to each create a unique animated look. Characters in vignettes discuss the meaning of human consciousness. An extraordinary film for questioning teens and a great film for discussion.

WALL-E (2008) G

> A salvage robot has been left alone on the abandoned, garbage-strewn Earth. A reconnaissance robot named EVE comes looking for proof that life has returned to earth so that humanity can return from space. The relationship between WALL-E and EVE is a love story between an ugly duckling and a swan, which has teen-aged appeal.

Waltz With Bashir [original title: *Vals Im Bashir*] (2008) R Israel

> Israeli documentarian Ari Folman, directed this powerful animated account of the massacre of thousands of Palestinian civilians in the Sabra and Shatila refugee camps during Israel's 1982 invasion of Lebanon.

Watchmen:The Complete Motion Comic (2009) NR

> The entire 12-episode story arc of the graphic novel has been turned into a new format called a "motion comic," which combines a voice cast and limited animation using the original artwork to produce an engrossing five-hour-long version.

Watchmen. Tales of the Black Freighter (2009) R

> Two short limited-animation films based on added material from the original *Watchman comic books*. This is, in effect, a bonus disc for fans of the movies and would be an additional purchase.

Yellow Submarine (1968) G United Kingdom/United States

> This film proves that animation and music can be timeless. The Blue Meanies invade Pepperland and Fred brings the Beatles to help defeat the enemy.

SELECTED ANIME TELEVISION SERIES

Most anime began as television series, and successful series spun off their own movie titles or feature-length episodes. Series have ongoing storylines, and beginning a series will commit you to collecting all the episodes. If you want to avoid this problem, look for the associated movie titles that have complete stories in themselves.

These anime television series are popular at our library, but are just examples of series that are available. You likely already have teen fans of most of these series in your community.

Ah! My Goddess
Appleseed
Basilisk
Bleach
Boogiepop Phantom
Chobits
Cowboy Bebop
Death Note
Dragonball Z
Fafner
FLCL
Fruits Basket
Full Metal Panic
Ghost in the Shell: Stand Alone Complex
Gundam Seed
Gunslinger Girl
Haibane Renmei
Hakugei: Legend of the Moby Dick
His and Hers Circumstances
Initial D
The Irresponsible Captain Tylor
Last Exile
Le Chevalier d'Eon
Macross
Neon Genesis Evangelion
Ninja Scroll
Noir
Planetes
Rahxephon
Ranma 1/2
Read or Die
Record of Lodoss War
Ruruoni Kenshi
Serial Experiments Lain
Trigun
Witch Hunter Robin

5

THE APPEAL
OF STRONG EMOTIONS:
SUGGESTED FILMS

Learning how to control one's emotions is a large part of growing up. However, teens are of an age where it is still perfectly acceptable for them to appreciate without reserve strong emotions such as humor and horror before the constraints of adulthood set in. Teens enjoy the adrenaline rush of being deeply scared as well as that of uninhibited laughter.

Most horror films and comedies are formulaic in nature, and as a result, they do not stimulate deep thought or complex emotions, making them great films for teens to watch casually on their own or in groups. Horror films are more likely to be date movies, since they provide an excuse for the girl to clutch the boy for protection. Comedies that rely on gross-out humor often provide male bonding experiences. (And just because these observations are dated, stereotypical, and sexist, doesn't mean they're not generally true.)

The formulaic structure of these films also improves their longevity, in that their appeal to teens may last longer than films that rely on star power alone, or on special effects that might age badly. (However, it must be noted that state-of-the-art special effects that turn cheesy with age can often edge a film that was not originally a comedy into the realm of the humorous.) Nevertheless, even though formulaic films tend to stand the test of time extremely well, often more successfully than other types of films, their value does not stem solely from their long-term relevance, but also from the one-time experience of intense fright or laughter that they provide to teen patrons. That said, some horror films and comedies are considered cinematic classics, and thus bear repeated viewing; examples include the original *Dawn of the Dead* or the truly classic *Duck Soup*.

Be assured that the films on this list, despite being horror films and comedies, nevertheless have artistic value that will keep your teen patrons coming back as adults. The laughs and chills these films deliver will also make your teen patrons recommend them to their friends.

HORROR AND SUSPENSE FILMS

Teens enjoy being scared, and Hollywood is aware of that fact. For this reason, mainstream horror films are primarily aimed at a teen audience. Furthermore, if a horror gimmick works, rest assured there will be a franchise of sequels based on the original premise. This means there is no shortage of material for you to choose from when adding horror and suspense films to your young adult collection.

However, when reviewing this material and deciding which films to include in your teen horror collection, it is critical that you exercise discretion. For example, you must be very clear about the ages you are actually expecting to serve. A teen collection aimed solely at junior high school students will have a vastly different approach to horror films than one aimed at high schoolers and younger college students. When selecting horror films for younger audiences in particular, you need to rely heavily on reviews, while paying close attention to the basis for the MPAA ratings the films have received.

Though it may seem obvious, the first point you should consider when reviewing horror films is that they inherently use violence and the threat of violence to shock the audience. For example, a steady threat of violence against women is one of the most standard, and even clichéd elements of horror films. Assess how the film treats violence and threats of violence, and how these issues are ultimately resolved. Evaluate how the film handles threats made against women.

- Does the female character show intelligence and courage?
- Is the threat against her crucial to the plotline or is it simply exploitative?
- Is there another character who diffuses some of the suspense, perhaps someone who provides some comic relief or who shows a marked tendency towards foolishness?

Ultimately, you can select films that downplay actual violence, but the threat of violence needs to be there in order for the film to fall into the horror genre. Reviews that discuss the level of violence and ratings that state concerns regarding violence can prove useful. Consult the Common Sense Media Web site discussed in the Introduction for more information about violence in films.

Incidentally, characters who act foolishly in the face of danger represent another clichéd element often found in horror films. Keep in mind that it wouldn't be a horror film if everyone acted sensibly.

The second point you should consider when reviewing horror films is that sexual metaphors appear in many forms, some obvious and some not so obvious. A vampire's blood lust is generally used to represent sexual lust; werewolves show men reduced to their most base desires and animal instincts; and witches provide a conduit through which to display women's sexual power. Couples who wander off to a secluded place to be intimate are often the first victims because they "deserve it," and sex also often comes into play as a motivation behind the actions of slasher-film villains. Additionally, horror films tend to play up sexual undertones to bolster their appeal, so pay close attention to ratings and reviews.

Some librarians understandably have second thoughts about including horror films in a teen collection because of these films' treatment of violence and sex. However, films that bring up violence and sex can often help teens work through many of their thoughts and feelings about these topics. Additionally, experiencing the feeling of terror from the safety of one's own home (or library) can be cathartic and helpful, as well as enjoyable. And while popularity should never be the only basis for the selection of items, horror films simply can't be avoided if you want to serve your teen population. Therefore, a categorical refusal to add this type of film to your teen collection will likely be counterproductive.

Both suspense and horror are what traditional storytellers would call jump stories: at some point during the story there is a moment when something so unforeseen or unexpected happens that the audience literally jumps. Horror movies are certainly full of moments when the audience is surprised, such as when the monster claims another victim. Even when the audience is anticipating these moments, skilled movie making can still create surprise.

Suspense films are usually subtler than most mainstream horror films. The expectation can be drawn out. In the classic suspense film *Wait Until Dark* (1967), the jump scene comes at the very end. In that film, three criminals trying to discover the whereabouts of a doll that contains drugs beset a blind woman. The heroine is completely in the dark, literally and figuratively, and for the audience who has been kept in suspense for the entire story, the payoff is very powerful. In suspense films, humans play the monsters hiding in the dark.

J-Horror: Japanese Horror Films

At the time of writing, Japanese horror films, or J-Horror, are exercising a strong influence over new Hollywood horror films. J-Horror represents something of a return to classic horror films since it doesn't rely on intensive special effects or the horror clichés of the last few decades. Japanese horror films rely on storytelling and a deft understanding of the psychological basis of creating fear. The threats of violence are suggested rather than shown, so each viewer can imagine his or her own perfect horror. Two excellent examples of J-Horror are the 1998 Japanese film *Ringu* and its 2002 American adaptation *The Ring*.

Japanese horror is reminiscent of classic horror films like the original *Psycho* or *Wait until Dark*. A J-Horror film typically opens with ordinary people living ordinary lives, but the viewer soon realizes that something is out of the ordinary after all. The films often come across as claustrophobic, with feelings of dread and anxiety created though the use of cinematic devices such as long silences and bleak empty spaces. Objects such as water stains or bloodstains appear where they should not be, and things often flash rapidly in and out of camera range. These cinematic tricks hint at terror without actually revealing it.

What to Look for When Selecting

- Select films with appropriate ratings, familiar directors and actors, or that come from major labels.
- Films made in the United States that go directly to DVD are usually of lower quality than ones that open in theaters (the same is not true of Japanese films.) If an American studio didn't think a horror film could make money in the movie theaters, it's probably not worth buying.
- Films that have not been submitted for ratings may have been rated R or X. If a feature film is not rated and you can't find reviews for it, you probably don't want it in your collection.
- Fan reviews often overlook details that might be critical in choosing a library collection. If you can't find professional reviews, watch the film, if possible.

- Older horror films are worth selecting.
- Listen to your teens.

Horror and Suspense Films

28 Days Later . . . (2002) R United Kingdom
28 Weeks Later (2007) R United Kingdom

> Laboratory animals carrying the dangerous Rage virus infect the human population when a group of animal activists free them from captivity. The sequel takes place seven months later, when the infected humans have starved to death, and another outbreak starts with a human carrier who is immune.

The *Alien* Franchise (1979 to 1997) R
AVP: Alien vs. Predator (2004) PG-13
AVPR: Aliens vs. Predator Requiem (2007) R

> These classic haunted-house-in-space films are uniquely creepy, and the monster in *Alien* is one of the scariest film monsters ever created. In *AVP*, the monster from *Alien* fights the monster from the 1987 Arnold Schwarzenegger film *Predator*.

Black Sheep (2006) NR New Zealand

> Killer sheep underlie the premise in this horror comedy that doesn't take itself too seriously and involves the audience in the joke.

The Blair Witch Project (1999) R
Book of Shadows: Blair Witch 2 (2000) R

> Three film students armed with a camera head into the woods of Bur-kettsville, Maryland in order to discover the truth about the Blair Witch. Notable for infusing some new devices into a cliché-ridden genre, the Blair Witch films made a lot of money for two relatively small, low-budget, independent films.

Blood and Chocolate (2007) PG-13

> A young female werewolf is sent to join an urban werewolf pack in order to breed with its leader. She runs into trouble when she falls in love with a human cartoonist. Annette Curtis Klause's vampire novel about teen werewolves didn't get the great cinematic treatment it deserved, but the film was popular nonetheless.

The Bourne Identity (2002) PG-13
The Bourne Supremacy (2004) PG-13
The Bourne Ultimatum (2007) PG-13

> In this trilogy, loosely based on the Robert Ludlum thrillers, the protagonist, Jason Bourne, suffers from amnesia and is persecuted everywhere he goes by friends and enemies alike. These three films chronicle Jason's journey to discover who he is and what his secrets are. Young people identify with Jason, who is played by Matt Damon, an actor already familiar to most teens.

Bram Stoker's Dracula (1992) R

> Francis Ford Coppola's highly stylized retelling of the classic novel is visually stunning and filled with passionate performances.

Brick (2005) R

> This film, a takeoff on hard-boiled detective mysteries, is set in a Southern California high school. After a young man finds his friend Emily dead, he sets off to discover how she died. Film noir for teens.

The Call of Cthulhu (2005) NR

> A dying man leaves his documents on the cult of Cthulhu to his great-nephew, who gradually succumbs to madness as he makes his own discoveries. A modern, silent black and white film adaptation of H. P. Lovecraft's 1926 classic horror story, this film was distributed by the H. P. Lovecraft Historical Society and was intended to look as though it were made in 1926 when the story was written. At only 48 minutes and available in 24 languages, it is perfect for Lovecraft fans everywhere.

Carrie (1976) R
Carrie (2002) TV 14 Made for television

> No one has ever felt the same about prom night since this story hit the theaters. Carrie is an outsider at her school and is only asked to prom so that she can be humiliated. Tables are turned as Carrie's telekinetic powers turn the night into a bloodbath. Stephen King's 1974 homage to the horrors of high school is still often referenced in general and popular writing and speech. The remake doesn't match the power of the original in any way.

The Cell (2000) R
The Cell 2 (2009) R

> When a serial killer slips into a coma, psychologist Catherine Deane (played by Jennifer Lopez) goes into his mind to find his last victim. Surreal, evocative images mesh with a first rate suspense plot. *Cell 2* doesn't measure up to the original.

Cloverfield (2008) PG-13

> Some rather dim friends in New York City try to escape a horrifying and indistinct monster. Fair monster fare.

The Covenant (2006) PG-13

> *The Covenant* is a dark story of teenage male witches attending a New England prep school.

The Craft (1996) R

> This film follows the lives and friendships of four teenage female witches in a Los Angeles Catholic prep school. It features an excellent soundtrack, which teens enjoy.

Cry Wolf (2005) PG-13

> Prep school friends play mind games on each other when there is a murder in the nearby woods. They begin spreading online rumors about The

Wolf, a made-up serial killer, to terrify their classmates. The tables turn when the students become the hunted and no one believes them.

Cube (1997) R
Cube 2: Hypercube (2002) R
Cube Zero (2004) R

In each of these films, a group of strangers find themselves in a maze of connecting cubes, with each cube containing a grisly trap or puzzle. The strangers must solve these puzzles or die. These are highly stylized films with great special effects.

Cursed [original title: *Cho kowai hanashi A: yami no karasu*] (2004) NR Japan

Malevolent spirits inhabit a convenience store with dire consequences. The film abounds with inside jokes (the cash register totals 666) and other references that horror fans will recognize and enjoy.

Cursed (2005) PG-13 United States

Two orphaned young adult siblings are forced to fight lycanthropy after a werewolf bites them when they stop to help an injured woman. Directed by Wes Craven of *Nightmare on Elm Street* fame.

Dark Water [original title: *Honogurai mizu no soko kara*] (2002) PG-13 Japan
Dark Water (2005) PG-13 United States

Due to a heated custody battle, a mother and her young daughter are forced to move into an affordable apartment. Supernatural phenomena start to occur: dark stains on the ceiling, sounds of running water from the unoccupied upstairs apartment, and the appearance of a strange spirit that befriends the young daughter. This American version is a remake of the original Japanese film.

Disturbia (2007) PG-13

Because of an incident during which he punched his teacher, teenage boy Kale is confined to his house with an ankle bracelet. He takes to spying on his neighbors and in doing so discovers that one of them appears to have killed someone. This remake of the classic Hitchcock film *Rear Window* is clever and suspenseful.

Eagle Eye (2008) PG-13

A single mother and a young man grieving the loss of his twin brother are forced to do the bidding of an omnipresent intelligence that knows everything that's going to happen.

The Evil Dead (1981) NC 17
Evil Dead II (1987) R
Army of Darkness (1992) R

Sam Raimi's *Evil Dead* trilogy, starring actor Bruce Campbell, goes for laughs over gore. As a result, the films are cult classics. In *The Evil Dead*, five young friends release a terrible evil during a weekend in a remote cabin in the woods, and only one, Ash, survives. In *Evil Dead II*, Ash goes back to the cabin with his girlfriend, plays a recording of *The Book of the*

Dead, and turns his girlfriend into a zombie. In *Army of Darkness,* Ash is sent to the 14th century to retrieve *The Book of the Dead,* which is his only way of returning to the present.

The Faculty (1998) R

The Faculty is a horror tale set in a high school where students start to notice the odd behavior of the teachers and soon discover that the teachers are aliens bent on making the students their victims.

Fear (1996) R

In this creepy thriller, a pretty teenage girl thinks the handsome charmer she meets at a party is the man of her dreams. However, the boy friend becomes dangerously obsessive. Stars Mark Wahlberg and Reese Witherspoon.

FeardotCom (2002) R

When a killer Web site begins implanting peoples' darkest and deepest fears into their brains, they start dying.

Final Destination (2000) R
Final Destination 2 (2003) R
Final Destination 3 (2006) R

People who survive accidents that should have killed them discover that death still waits for them.

Freeway (1996) R

This film is a very dark and deranged adaptation of the Little Red Riding Hood story. Stars Reese Witherspoon and Kiefer Sutherland.

The *Friday the 13*th Franchise (1980 to 2003) R

Deformed as a result of hydrocephalus, Jason Voorhees was always teased by other children. After drowning as a result of neglect by summer camp counselors, Jason rises to avenge himself on anyone who gets in his way. A must see for horror fans, the first film of this series was groundbreaking and began an entire movement of teen terror films, including 10 sequels to the original film. Jason Voorhees forever made hockey masks a staple for Halloween costumes. Jason eventually meets fellow horror icon Freddy, from the *Nightmare on Elm Street* franchise, in the film *Freddy vs. Jason* (2003) R. A remake of the original is due for release in 2009.

The Frighteners (1996) R

After the success of the *Lord of the Rings* trilogy, this early film by Peter Jackson will undoubtedly be in demand. This film tells the story of a psychic detective who uses his ability to contact the dead to stop a serial killer. Funny and entertaining.

Going to Pieces: The Rise and Fall of the Slasher Film (2007) NR Documentary

This wide-ranging and insightful documentary will appeal to all horror fans.

The Grudge (2004) PG-13 United States
The Grudge 2 (2006) PG-13 United States
Ju-on (2000) R Japan
Ju-on 2 (2000) R Japan

A ghost haunts a young woman who is caring for an old woman in a cursed house. Director Takashi Shimizu, who directed the original *Ju-on* franchise as well as the Hollywood remakes, uses unusual camera work and decidedly scary devices in this set of films.

The *Halloween* Franchise (1978 to 2007) R

Though sometimes credited with spawning the slasher film genre, the original John Carpenter film is relatively nonviolent. The storyline follows the urban legend of the babysitter who receives mysterious phone calls before discovering that the calls are coming from within the house. The main character, Michael Myers, has become a modern horror monster icon, starring in eight follow up films to the original. Rob Zombie, a speed metal musician and horror movie director, remade the original *Halloween* in 2007.

Hangman's Curse (2003) PG-13

This film is based on Frank Peretti's Christian teen novel *The Veritas Project: Hangman's Curse*. A family of investigators goes undercover in a high school to stop demons. This horror film with decent people trying to stop evil is suitable for younger teens.

The Host [original title: *Gwoemul*] (2006) R South Korea

A monster caused by human pollution rises out of the Seoul River and makes the mistake of messing with the eccentric Park family. One of the top grossing films in Korea, this is a great new take on a basic and overused plot line.

Hostel (2005) R
Hostel: Part II (2007) R

American students go to Europe to have a good time and find themselves captives of a business whose clients pay for the opportunity to torture and kill victims. Both of these films are above average horror films, but are very violent.

I Am Legend (2007) PG-13

Virologist Robert Neville lives in New York City and is the apparent sole survivor of a virus that turns people into zombie-like monsters. The film follows Neville's effort to perfect an antidote. Will Smith starring as Neville makes this film great. Based on the 1954 science fiction novella by Richard Matheson.

I Know What You Did Last Summer (1997) R
I Still Know What You Did Last Summer (1998) R
I'll Always Know What You Did Last Summer (2006) R

This film and the sequels are very loose adaptations of Lois Duncan's thriller about four teenagers trying to cover up a fatal hit and run car accident.

I Know Who Killed Me (2007) R

> Lindsay Lohan plays Aubrey, a high school student whose disappearance leads police to suspect that she is a victim of a serial killer. A week later she turns up seriously injured, claiming she is not who everyone thinks she is, and that the real Aubrey is still in danger.

The In Crowd (2000) PG-13

> A disturbed young woman gets a job at a posh country club, becomes involved with the in crowd, and things soon become deadly.

The Invisible (2007) PG-13

> A remake of the 2002 Swedish film *Den Osynlige*, this film tells the story of a teenage boy who finds himself trapped in the form of an invisible being after he is beaten nearly to death. Not quite alive, but not yet dead, the main character has a limited amount of time to find his unconscious body and right the wrong done to him.

Let the Right One In [original title: *Låt den rätte komma in*] (2008) R Sweden

> Twelve-year-old Oscar is a lonely and bullied kid who befriends Eli, a mysterious girl who shows up one night outside his apartment building. This atmospheric and moving vampire film is really a love story between the two adolescents.

The Lost Boys (1987) R

> Teen Michael Emerson moves to coastal town Santa Carla, California with his mother and little brother. He is not there long before he starts making all the wrong friends, including vampires. This classic is considered by many to be the quintessential teen vampire film.

The Messengers (2007) PG-13

> When her family moves from Chicago to North Dakota, teenager Jess becomes the victim of strange occurrences tied in with the disappearance of the house's previous owners.

The *Nightmare on Elm Street* Franchise (1984 to 2003) R

> The disturbed product of a brutal rape, Freddy Krueger is burnt alive by the citizens of a small Ohio town after he begins killing children. He takes his revenge from beyond the grave by continuing to kill children in their dreams. Wes Craven's first film in the Freddy Krueger legacy is an entertaining but disturbing film, and is followed by a series of seven disappointing sequels. The idea of not being safe even in your dreams is a scary one. Like Jason Vorhees and Michael Myers, Freddy Krueger is an iconic horror character.

Night of the Living Dead (1968) NR Black and white
Dawn of the Dead (1978) R
Day of the Dead (1985) NR
Night of the Living Dead (1990) R
Dawn of the Dead (2004) R
Land of the Dead (2005) R

Night of the Living Dead 3D (2006) R
Diary of the Dead (2007) R
Day of the Dead (2008) R

George Romero's original zombie film, *Night of the Living Dead*, was done on a shoestring budget, but was nevertheless wildly successful. The recent film, *Diary of the Dead*, is an extraordinarily good film and belongs in every horror film collection.

One Missed Call [original title: Chakushin ari] (2003) R Japan
One Missed Call (2008) PG-13 United States

A killing force chooses its victims based on their cell phone address books. The American remake is much less violent and scary than the J-Horror original.

Pulse [original title: *Kairo*] (2001) R Japan
Pulse (2006) PG-13 United States
Pulse 2: Afterlife (2008) R United States
Pulse 3 (2008) R United States

The original film is Kiyoshi Kurosawa's cult success about a series of suicides and disappearances that are all somehow linked to computers. Atmospheric and grim, it is a modern horror classic. Sadly, the American remakes and sequels are not as good, though they are likely to be popular.

The Return (2006) PG-13

Terrifying nightmares draw a young woman to a town where another young woman was brutally murdered.

The Ring (2002) PG-13 United States
The Ring 2 (2005) PG-13 United States
Rasen (1998) NR Japan
Ringu (1998) NR Japan
Ringu 2 (1999) NR Japan
Ringu 0: Basudei [*Birthday*] (2000) NR Japan

Based on a series of novels by Koji Suzuki, this Japanese horror film series and the corresponding American remakes are some of the most terrifying films ever made. The premise: if a certain videotape is watched, the viewer will receive a phone call stating that he or she will die in seven days. The American version of the original *Ringu* was one of the most commercially successful of the J-Horror remakes.

Scary Movie (2000) R
Scary Movie 2 (2001) R
Scary Movie 3 (2003) PG-13
Scary Movie 4 (2006) PG-13

These satires of teen slasher films as done by the Wayans brothers aren't all that scary, and they're not all that funny either, but some horror fans enjoy the humor and references to other films.

Scream (1996) R
Scream 2 (1997) R

Scream 3 (2000) R

> Wes Craven's *Scream* opens with a 10-minute clip featuring Drew Barrymore that encompasses every cliché of the slasher film genre. The main plot continues with the investigation of earlier deaths by a cast of characters who are hip enough about horror films to satirize them even as the body count escalates. These are modern horror classics.

Shaun of the Dead (2004) R United Kingdom

> A loser salesman at a local electronics store, Shaun and his game-fanatic roommate Ed wake up to find everyone around them turning into zombies. Hilarious both as a satire of zombie films and in its own right.

Signs (2002) PG-13

> *Signs* is M. Night Shyamalan's thriller about a widower, his brother, and his children facing a race of aliens that have landed on Earth.

The Sixth Sense (1999) PG-13

> *The Sixth Sense* was an instant classic and M. Night Shyamalan's breakthrough film. A young boy who sees dead people meets a child psychologist who devotes himself to helping him. Eerie and scary, this film is a modern classic with a surprising twist.

Spiral (2007) PG-13

> A portrait painter with a mysterious past, Mason meets a charming new woman at work, but the romance falters when Mason begins to act oddly.

Stormbreaker (2006) PG

> Fourteen-year-old Alex becomes an agent for M16, the British secret intelligence service, when his uncle and guardian, also an agent, is killed. Based on the Alex Rider books by Anthony Horowitz.

Swimfan (2002) PG-13

> A teenage swimming champion who has it all begins to lose it all when he falls for the new girl in town after she becomes his obsessive fan.

The Texas Chain Saw Massacre (1974) R
The Texas Chainsaw Massacre 2 (1986) NR
Leatherface: Texas Chainsaw Massacre III (1990) R
The Return of the Texas Chainsaw Massacre (1994) R
The Texas Chainsaw Massacre (2003) R
The Texas Chainsaw Massacre: The Beginning (2006) R

> In the first movie, five young friends traveling rural Texas make the mistake of running out of gas in front of the home of crazed killer, Leatherface, who hunts them down one by one. Tobe Hooper's original indie black and white cult classic wasn't as violent as its sequels.

Underworld (2003) R
Underworld: Evolution (2006) R
Underworld: The Rise of the Lycans (2009) R

> In a world where their races are at war with each other, beautiful vampire Selene falls in love with werewolf Michael. Fabulous special effects highlight the unusual paranormal plot.

Urban Legend (1998) R
Urban Legends: Final Cut (2000) R
Urban Legends: Bloody Mary (2005) R

> These films incorporate urban legends into their formulaic horror film plots. *Urban Legends: Final Cut* is a slasher movie set in a film school, where the prize for students exposing themselves to horrible death is a film award.

The Village (2004) PG-13

> Unknown and largely unseen monsters referred to as "those we do not speak of" frighten villagers living in the deep woods but don't deliver the scares viewers hope for. M. Night Shyamalan's name will make this film popular among teens.

WarGames (1983) PG

> A teen hacks into a computer and finds a game called Global Thermo-nuclear War, only to discover that he has hacked into the Pentagon's War Room. The suspenseful and believable plot has a great twist at the end. Starring Matthew Broderick and Ally Sheedy.

COMEDY FILMS

When librarians of a certain age think of teen comedies, they may think of films like *Porky's* or *American Pie* that rely on sophomoric gross out humor to appeal to their audiences. However, today's teens are more sophisticated in ways that prior generations were not, and that sophistication shows in modern film humor.

Because of the amount and types of media children are exposed to by the time they become teens, today's teens have developed awareness of the marketers targeting them. Since teens are aware of attempts to manipulate them, advertisers are learning to do their manipulating in a more amusing, tongue-in-cheek way. Films and television still influence how teens sound, look, act, and dress, but teens nevertheless treat the media with a healthy suspicion, and films aimed at teens have become better for it.

Satire is a common attribute of humor today. The media began aiming satirical humor at younger pop culture consumers in the 1950s, when *Mad Magazine* made its debut appearance in 1952. This trend continued throughout the 1960s and 1970s as the magazine continued to cultivate an impressive fan base. *Mad Magazine* is often credited with starting a tradition of subversive media criticism that opened the door for outfits such as *National Lampoon* and *Saturday Night Live*.

Early exposures to satire helps teens develop a sophisticated approach to what they read, hear, and see in the popular media. However, for satire to work as humor, the consumer must be aware of what is being satirized and be able to separate the context from the content to appreciate the joke.

Humor works especially well for teens when it makes fun of authorities. The protagonists in most of these types of comedies are antiheroes whose problems teens can sympathize with. The common theme is one of the underdog, or "revenge of the nerds," and in such films the humor can be very earthy. Underdogs overcoming obstacles is a winning storyline in a teen film. Another winning storyline is the use of misfit characters in recognizable settings making embarrassing mistakes or pointing out the absurdity of normal situations. These scenarios often mirror situations that teens find themselves in, and as a result the scenarios can be both entertaining and reassuring to young people.

What to Look for When Selecting

- Teens are often just looking for a laugh, so a shallow vapid film isn't necessarily a bad choice as long as the characters are treated compassionately and any unfair treatment is balanced out in the end.
- If a film starring a particular comedian works for teens at your library, consider adding all the works by that comedian. Films starring alumni from *Saturday Night Live* and *SCTV* are usually good selections whether or not the films garner favorable reviews or not. Many of these films are classic comedies despite their age or the age of their stars. Any connection a starring actor has with *Saturday Night Live*, be it as host, guest, or cast member, is a good basis for including a comedy film, no matter how badly it is critically reviewed. Consider adding movies that are not comedies by these actors as well.
  - Dan Ackroyd: *The Blues Brothers; Ghost Busters; Ghostbusters II*
  - Drew Barrymore: *Never Been Kissed; Charlie's Angels; Charlie's Angels: Full Throttle*
  - John Belushi: *Animal House; The Blues Brothers*
  - Jack Black: *School of Rock; Nacho Libre; Be Kind, Rewind; Tropic Thunder*
  - John Candy: *Uncle Buck; Spaceballs*
  - Dana Carvey: *Wayne's World; Wayne's World 2*
  - Cedric the Entertainer: *Barbershop; Barbershop 2; Code Name: The Cleaner; Be Cool*
  - Michael Cera: *Superbad; Juno; Nick and Norah's Infinite Playlist*
  - Chevy Chase: *National Lampoon's Vacation; Caddyshack*
  - John Cho: *Harold and Kumar Go To White Castle; Harold and Kumar Escape from Guantanamo Bay; American Wedding*

- Billy Crystal: *When Harry Met Sally*; *City Slickers*; *Princess Bride*
- Jane Curtin: *The Coneheads*; *The Librarian: Quest for the Spear*; *The Librarian: Return to King Solomon's Mines*; *The Librarian: Curse of the Judas Chalice*
- Cameron Diaz: *There's Something About Mary*; *Shrek, Shrek 2,* and *Shrek the Third*; *What Happens in Vegas*
- Robert Downey, Jr.: *Iron Man*; *Tropic Thunder*
- Kirsten Dunst: *Spider-Man*; *Bring It On*
- Tina Fey: *Mean Girls*; *Baby Mama*; *Dick*; *Drop Dead Gorgeous*
- Jimmy Fallon: *Almost Famous*; *The Year of Getting to Know Us*
- Chris Farley: *Tommy Boy*; *Black Sheep*; *Beverly Hills Ninja,*
- Will Ferrell: *Elf*; *Old School*; *Blades of Glory*; *Semi-Pro*
- Christopher Guest: *Waiting For Guffman*; *The Princess Bride*
- Alyson Hannigan: *Date Movie*; *American Pie 1 & 2*; *American Wedding*
- Anne Hathaway: *The Princess Diaries*; *Ella Enchanted*; *Get Smart*
- Jon Heder: *Napoleon Dynamite*; *Blades of Glory*; *School for Scoundrels*; *Benchwarmers*
- Emile Hirsch: *Speed Racer*; *The Girl Next Door*
- Kate Hudson: *Raising Helen*; *You*; *Me and Dupree*; *How to Lose a Guy in 10 Days*; *Almost Famous*
- Chris Kattan: *Corky Romano*; *A Night At the Roxbury*; *Benchwarmers*
- Ashton Kutcher: *Dude, Where's My Car?*; *What Happens in Vegas*
- Queen Latifah: *Bringing Down the House*; *Taxi*; *Beauty Shop*
- Lucy Liu: *Charlie's Angels* and *Charlie's Angels: Full Throttle*; *Kung Fu Panda*; *Kill Bill*
- Lindsay Lohan: *Mean Girls*; *Confessions of a Teenage Drama Queen*
- Rob Lowe: *Wayne's World*; *Tommy Boy*; *Austen Powers: The Spy Who Shagged Me*
- Steve Martin: *The Jerk*; *Dead Men Don't Wear Plaid*; *Man with Two Brains*
- Mo'Nique: *Phat Girlz*; *Hair Show*
- Rick Moranis: *Ghostbusters*; *Honey I Shrunk the Kids*
- Tracy Morgan: *First Sunday*; *30 Years to Life*
- Eddie Murphy: *48 Hours*; *Beverly Hills Cop*; *Coming to America*
- Bill Murray: *Groundhog Day*; *Ghostbusters*; *Caddyshack*
- Mike Myers: *Wayne's World*; *Austin Powers*; *The Love Guru*

- Bob Newhart: *Legally Blond 2: Red, White & Blond; Elf; The Librarian: Quest for the Spear; The Librarian: Return to King Solomon's Mines; The Librarian: Curse of the Judas Chalice*
- Laraine Newman: *Invaders from Mars; Jimmy Neutron: Boy Genius*
- Catherine O'Hara: *Home Alone; Best in Show; A Mighty Wind*
- Kal Penn: *Harold and Kumar Go To White Castle; Harold and Kumar Escape from Guantanamo; The Namesake*
- Amy Poehler: *Shrek; Baby Mama*
- Christina Ricci: *The Addams Family; Penelope; Speed Racer*
- Chris Rock: *Dogma; The Longest Yard*
- Winona Ryder: *Beetlejuice; Heathers; Mermaids*
- Adam Sandler: *Big Daddy; Waterboy; Click; Spanglish*
- Rob Schneider: *Deuce Bigelow; Benchwarmers; The Animal*
- Seann William Scott: *American Pie 1 & 2; Mr. Woodcock; The Dukes of Hazzard; Role Models*
- Martin Short: *Three Amigos; Father of the Bride*
- Alicia Silverstone: *Clueless; Beauty Shop*
- David Spade: *Beverly Hills Ninja; Dickie Roberts; Benchwarmers*
- Ben Stiller: *Zoolander; Meet the Parents; Tropic Thunder*
- Justin Timberlake: *The Love Guru; Alpha Dog*
- Marlon Wayans: *Scary Movie; Scary Movie 2; White Chicks; Dance Flick; Little Man; Norbit*
- Keenen Wayans: *Scary Movie; Dance Flick*
- Gene Wilder: *Young Frankenstein*
- Luke Wilson: *Rushmore; Bottle Rocket; Old School; Idiocracy; Legally Blonde; Legally Blonde: Red, White & Blonde; Vacancy*
- Owen Wilson: *Drillbit Taylor; Darjeeling Limited; Wedding Crashers; Zoolander*
- Reese Witherspoon: *Legally Blonde; Legally Blonde: Red, White & Blonde,; Election; Little Nicky*

Comedy Films

100 Girls (2000) R

College freshman geek Matthew meets the girl of his dreams in an elevator during a blackout but doesn't learn her name. Matthew is determined to find her, but the only clue he has, aside from her discarded underwear, is that she lives in a girls' dorm.

Accepted (2006) PG-13

After suburban teen Bartleby Gaines is rejected by eight colleges, he creates a phony college called South Harmon Institute of Technology to fool his parents. Hilarity ensues.

Animal House (1978) R

This ultimate fraternity/sorority college film starring a young John Belushi is a classic. The *National Lampoon* franchise of films includes more than 30 titles. The following are among the most well known:

- *Christmas Vacation* (1989) PG-13
- *European Vacation* (1985) R
- *Going the Distance* (2004) R
- *Senior Trip* (1995) R
- *Vacation* (1983) R
- *Van Wilder* (2002) R
- *Van Wilder 2:* The Rise of Taj (2006) R
- *Vegas Vacation* (1997) PG

Another Gay Movie (2006) NR
Another Gay Sequel: Gays Gone Wild (2008) NR

Four gay high school teens vow to lose their virginity before they graduate in this spoof of teen coming-of-age movies. The sequel is not recommended but you may have teens who'll like it.

Aquamarine (2006) PG

Based on the Alice Hoffman novel, this is a sweet movie about two 13-year-old girls who befriend a mermaid.

Austin Powers: International Man of Mystery (1997) PG-13
Austin Powers: The Spy Who Shagged Me (1999) PG-13
Austin Powers in Goldmember (2002) PG-13

After being frozen for 30 years, British secret agent Austin Powers is defrosted to fight his newly-defrosted nemesis Dr. Evil. The Austin Powers series of films satirize both the spy film genre and 1960s culture. Mike Myers created many pop cultural icons in these films, including Dr. Evil and Mini Me.

Be Kind, Rewind (2008) PG-13

Mike, a clerk in a video store, and his friend Jerry accidentally erase all the movies, then decide to recreate them all themselves, with hilarious results.

Bill & Ted's Excellent Adventure (1989) PG
Bill and Ted's Bogus Journey (1991) PG

> Valley boys Bill and Ted, fated to become future world leaders, are given a little help from George Carlin as they travel through time to save the world.

Blades of Glory (2007) PG-13

> Will Ferrell and Jon Heder portray Olympic ice skaters, who, stripped of their medals, come together to compete as a team.

Borat: Cultural Learnings of America for Make Benefit Glorious Nation of Kazakhstan (2006) R United Kingdom/United States

> This is Sacha Baron Cohen's hilarious and controversial film about Borat Sagdiyev, a fictional television reporter from Kazakhstan, and Azamat, his producer. The film follows their travels across the country as they film a documentary about American society, skewering American mores and culture along the way.

Buffy the Vampire Slayer (1992) PG-13

> Valley girl Buffy Summers is a fashion-obsessed cheerleader, so she's dismayed to discover that she's The Chosen One, destined to hunt and slay vampires. Writer Josh Whedon's vision for Buffy Summers was hijacked, so the television series is much better than the film, but the film is still worth watching for a laugh or two.

Can't Hardly Wait (1998) PG-13

> Before he leaves for college, Preston decides to declare his feelings for Amanda, the girl he has cared about since he was a freshman in high school.

College Road Trip (2008) G

> Martin Lawrence takes his daughter to visit prospective colleges in this somewhat dreary but ever-popular comedy.

Confessions of a Teen Age Drama Queen (2004) PG

> Based on Dyan Sheldon's book, this film is about a new girl in town who gains a best friend and a choice role in the school theater production, but not without a lot of drama first.

Clerks (1994) R
Clerks II (2006) R

> Filmmaker Kevin Smith made the original black and white film for $27,575 and created a cult classic. The sequel is set several years later, with the original lead characters working in a fast food hamburger chain.

Clueless (1995) PG-13

> Alicia Silverstone shines as a rich Beverly Hills high school student who spends her time trying to fix up other peoples' lives. Loosely based on Jane Austen's *Emma*.

College (2008) R

Ribald and racy comedy about three high school seniors who go on a college visit weekend expecting to have a great time but getting hazed by a fraternity instead.

Crossroads (2002) PG-13

Britney Spears's big screen debut is a road trip movie about three childhood friends who reunite on a trip to California. Until Britney loses her star appeal, this will be a popular film despite being a so-so movie.

Dance Movie (2009) PG-13

This is a spoof of teen dance movies like *Save the Last Dance for Me* and *High School Musical*.

Date Movie (2006) PG-13

This is a spoof on teen date movies and romantic comedies. There are too many teen movies being spoofed to list them all.

D.E.B.S. (2004) PG-13

Teen girls are recruited into a secret government organization to become assassins in this campy, clever, and funny tale. In a plot twist, two girls ordered to kill each other fall in love.

Dick (1999) PG-13

During the Watergate scandal of Richard Nixon's presidency, two girls on a tour of the White House stumble on a room full of suspicious documents and cash.

Disaster Movie (2008) PG-13

A group of 20-somethings struggle to survive a catalog of disaster-movie cliché catastrophes on one very bad night.

Dogma (1999) R

Two outcast angels discover a loophole in the Catholic Canon that will permit them to reenter heaven, but will cause the end of the world if they do. Meanwhile, the forces of good try to stop them. Sacred and profane, the ideas put forth in this Kevin Smith film will undoubtedly interest teens.

Duck Season [original title: *Temporada de patos*] (2004) R Mexico Black and white

Two 14-year-old boys spend a lazy Sunday afternoon together playing videogames when a pizza delivery guy and a neighbor intrude. This film won 11 Ariel Awards, the Mexican equivalent of Academy Awards.

Duck Soup (1933) NR Black and white

Groucho Marx plays Rufus T. Firefly, head of the fictional country Freedonia. Fellow Marx Brothers, Chico, Harpo, and Zeppo join him in satirizing war, politics, and just about everything that comes along. Brilliant and hilarious, this comedy classic is worth trying out in your collection.

Dude, Where's My Car? (2000) PG-13

> Ashton Kutcher and Seann William Scott play two idiots facing the worst "day after" in history.

Election (1999) R

> Matthew Broderick plays a high school teacher who attempts to undermine the election for class president in order to foil the know-it-all girl, played by Reese Witherspoon, who is running for the job. A funny and biting satire.

Epic Movie (2007) PG-13

> This film satirizes many popular epic films, including the *Harry Potter* series, the *Pirates of the Caribbean* trilogy, and the *Chronicles of Narnia* films.

Ferris Bueller's Day Off (1986) PG-13

> Ferris Bueller, a high school senior, plays hooky with two friends in Chicago while his principal and older sister try to catch him in the act. Another classic teen film by John Hughes.

The Film Crew: The Giant of Marathon (2007) NR
The Film Crew: Hollywood After Dark (2007) NR
The Film Crew: Killers from Space (2007) NR
The Film Crew: Wild Women of Wongo (2007) NR

> Some of the original creators of the television show *Mystery Science Theater 3000* reunited in these films to make smart remarks and jokes while watching B movies.

Freaky Friday (2003) PG

> This terrific updated version of the Mary Rodgers novel is modern, fresh, and funny. Stars Jamie Lee Curtis and Lindsay Lohan play an overworked psychologist and her teen daughter who trade bodies after eating cookies given to them by an old woman.

Fronterz (2004) NR

> Three classically trained young black actors can't get work, so they reinvent themselves as a rap group. A scathing satire on several levels.

Get Over It (2001) PG-13

> A very loose adaptation of William Shakespeare's *A Midsummer's Night Dream* set in the world of high school theater production. When Allison dumps Berke, he joins the cast of the school musical to win her back. He's horrible onstage, but when his friend's sister helps him improve, things begin to change in more ways than one.

Go (1999) R

> This film chronicles the crazy adventures of 18-year-old Ronna when she and two of her friends decide to go out and party. This film is edgy, unique, and very well done.

The Girl Next Door (2004) R

> Successful but unpopular high school senior Matthew can't believe his luck when his dream girl moves in next door. The girl does have her

faults, however—for one thing, she used to be a porn star. A sweet, silly, and basically harmless comedy.

Harold & Kumar Go to White Castle (2004) R
Harold & Kumar Escape from Guantanamo Bay (2008) R

In the original film, a Korean American and his Indian American room-mate decide to take a road trip that drops them into an American wonder-land of mad drug dealers, weird cops, and a screwball tow truck driver. The sequel offers more of the same.

Heathers (1989) R

Although she's always been friends with a clique of girls all of whom are named Heather, Veronica soon comes to realize that she actually hates them. When Veronica teams up with a Machiavellian boy named JD, the film shifts into a dark, metaphysical, and funny view of teen relation-ships. This film is still potent nearly 20 years after its release.

High School High (1996) PG-13

A teacher, played by Jon Lovitz, transfers from a posh academy to inner-city Marion Barry High School, the toughest high school in the world.

Holes (2003) PG

In this able film adaptation of Louis Sachar's novel of the same name, a group kids in a juvenile facility are forced to dig holes because the war-den is searching for a lost treasure.

House Bunny (2008) PG-13

When ex-Playboy bunny Shelly finds herself out of work, she ends up as house mother to the Zeta Alpha Zeta sorority and finds her true calling in life. Like *Legally Blonde, House Bunny* is a better movie than expected.

Idiocracy (2006) R

As a result of a hibernation experiment gone wrong, Joe Bauers wakes up in 2505 only to discover that he is the smartest guy alive. A dystopian tale mocking popular culture.

Jay and Silent Bob Strike Back (2001) R

Jay and Bob, the drug dealers from the *Clerks* films, travel to Hollywood to stop production of a film based on a comic book about them. This film is lewd and socially unacceptable, but hilarious nonetheless.

Joe's Apartment (1996) PG-13

Joe's Apartment is MTV's film production debut about a nice guy who moves into an atrocious New York apartment.

John Tucker Must Die (2006) PG-13

While basketball star John Tucker secretly dates three different girls and claims each of them is the one, the girls discover the truth and plot revenge.

Just One of the Guys (1985) PG-13

Beautiful girl Terri transforms into guy Terry in order to write an under-cover report on gender bias at her high school. In a sweet and eye open-ing story, Terri ultimately learns what's really important in her life.

Kids in America (2005) PG-13

Typical high school problems such as administrative intolerance, first love, and the school play are showcased in this great film that shows what teen movies ought to be like. Smart and clever, the actors look like real high school students, and the events and issues are credible.

Kung Pow: Enter the Fist (2002) PG-13

Director and star Steve Oedekerk takes 1970s martial arts film *Tiger & Crane Fists* and inserts his character along with new dialog and scenes. The hero, the Chosen One, was an infant when Master Pain killed his parents and now he understands a quest for revenge.

Legally Blonde (2001) PG-13
Legally Blonde 2: Red, White & Blonde (2003) PG-13

A Bel Air sorority princess gets into Harvard Law School to win back her boyfriend, but discovers that she has a lot to offer in her own right. In the sequel, she takes on Washington politics.

Love Com (2006) NR Japan

Based on the manga series by Aya Nakahara, this is the hilarious story of the rocky road to love between a very tall girl, Risa, and a short boy, Otani.

Love and Death (1975) PG

Woody Allen's satire on Russian epic novels, classic European films, and just about every philosopher of note is the story of Russian coward, Boris Grushenko, and his love Sonia, who decide to assassinate Napoleon.

Mystery Science Theater 3000: the Movie [Also known as *MST3K: The Movie*] (1996)
      PG-13

Earthbound Dr. Clayton Forrester forces Mike and his sidekick robots, all of whom are stranded on a spaceship, to watch the 1954 cult science fiction film *This Island Earth*. Mike and the robots wisecrack during the movie from their screening room. This stand-alone film does not oblige you to buy all the episodes of the television show (which is important for those libraries whose collection policy requires the purchase of an entire television series).

Nacho Libre (2006) PG

Disappointing Jack Black film in which he plays a Mexican priest who becomes a masked wrestler to raise money for his flock. Very popular film with teens, especially with Hispanic teens.

Never Been Kissed (1999) PG-13

A 25-year-old reporter goes back to high school undercover as part of her research for a piece on modern high schools and gets a chance to relive her adolescence.

The New Guy (2002) PG-13

DJ Qualls plays a perennial loser, so embarrassed at his high school that he leaves and goes to a different one to create a new identity for himself.

Nick and Norah's Infinite Playlist (2008) R

> This movie, based on the young adult novel of the same name by Rachael Cohn and David Levithan, is an entertaining comedy of errors romp through New York City night life.

Not Another Teen Movie (2001) R

> On a dare, the Student Council president agrees to turn loser art major Janey into a prom queen. A satire of many teen films, this film has some truly funny moments.

Old School (2003) R

> A pale imitation of *Animal House* featuring Will Ferrell, Luke Wilson, and Vince Vaughan, who portray three friends trying to relive their college days. The casting makes this a very popular film.

Orange County (2002) PG-13

> Surfer Shaun discovers a book on the beach that changes his life, and he decides he wants to get into Stanford. Unfortunately, his transcripts get lost, and he has to figure out how to get into college despite his crazy friends and even crazier family. Starring Colin Hanks and Jack Black.

Paul Blart: Mall Cop (2009) PG

> Paul Blart rises (after a fashion) to the occasion when his shopping mall is taken over by a criminal gang.

Pee Wee's Big Adventure (1985) PG
Big Top Pee Wee (1988) PG

> In *tour de force* performances by comedian Paul Reubens, quirky Pee Wee lives according to his own unique standards. When his beloved bicycle is stolen, he embarks on a adventure to get it back. In the sequel, a circus is stranded at Pee Wee's farm. The original was directed by Tim Burton.

The Princess Bride (1987) PG

> This film is Rob Reiner's classic comedy about the lovely Buttercup finding her one true love in stable boy Westley. Based on William Goldman's novel, this film is about as good as a film can get.

The Princess Diaries (2001) G
The Princess Diaries 2: Royal Engagement (2004) G

> Fifteen-year-old San Francisco teen Mia Thermopolis learns that she is the heir to the throne of Genovia and that she must return there to be taught how to be a princess by her grandmother. In the sequel, she finds she must marry a prince. Anne Hathaway shines in these film adaptations of Meg Cabot's popular books.

Porky's (1982) R
Porky's II: The Next Day (1983) R
Porky's Revenge (1985) R

> A group of high school guys spend all their time sitting in a diner plotting ways to have sex. While the films are dated, their lewd and crude humor still appeals to many teens.

Revenge of the Nerds (1984) R
Revenge of the Nerds II: Nerds In Paradise (1987) PG-13
Revenge of the Nerds III: The Next Generation (1992) NR Made for television
Revenge of the Nerds IV: Nerds In Love (1994) NR Made For television

> The original film in this series is a funny and sweet classic that sets the pattern for other films. It chronicles the adventures of a lovable group of underdog nerds who suffer for a while but triumph in the end. The sequels are not as good as the original.

Role Models (2008) R

> When two young men, one a spokesman for and the other a costume-wearing mascot for an energy drink lose control and tell a cafeteria full of teens about how great drugs are, both are sentenced to community service in a program that warns kids off drugs.

Rush Hour (1998) PG-13
Rush Hour 2 (2001) PG-13
Rush Hour 3 (2007) PG-13

> A manic Los Angeles cop is forced to pair up with a policeman from Hong Kong to fight crime both in the United States and abroad. Chris Tucker and Jackie Chan star.

School of Rock (2003) PG-13

> When Jack Black is kicked out of his own band, he takes his roommate's place as a substitute teacher in a prep school to make money. He decides to form a rock band with his junior high school students so he can play in a Battle of the Bands concert against his old band.

She's All That (1999) PG-13

> When his girlfriend dumps him, popular Zach accepts a bet that he can't turn a geeky loner artist into an acceptable prom date.

She's the Man (2006) PG-13

> After the girls' soccer team at her school is disbanded, Viola disguises herself as a male and gets on the boys' team at her brother's school. An adept, modern version of *Twelfth Night*.

The Sisterhood of the Traveling Pants (2005) PG
Sisterhood of the Traveling Pants 2 (2008) PG-13

> Four girlfriends find a magical pair of blue jeans that fit all of them perfectly. Over the summer, the girls mail the jeans to each other and have adventures. In the sequel, the girls' adventures with the jeans continue as they go on to college. This nicely filmed version of Ann Brashares's novel is a PG version of a PG-13 book.

Slap Her . . . She's French [alternate title: *She Gets What She Wants*] (2002) PG-13

> Starla, a cheerleader and the most popular girl in her Texas high school, has her life destroyed when a French exchange student, Genevieve LePlouff, moves in with her family and gets everyone to like her more than Starla.

Sleeper (1973) PG

In this Woody Allen satire on science fiction, Miles Monroe, health food store owner from Greenwich Village in 1973, wakes after 200 years of cryogenic sleep to find that a Big Brother-like leader is in control.

So I Married an Axe Murderer (1993) PG-13

Saturday Night Live alum Mike Myers's portrays a man who has had the worst series of relationships; but in the end, finally finds his true love.

Summer School (1987) PG-13

This little sleeper of a comedy tells the story of a laconic teacher, played by Mark Harmon, and the crazy and troubled students in his summer school class. Smart, sweet, and funny.

Superbad (2007) R

Best friends Seth and Evan plan to lose their virginity at the last party before they leave for college. Unfortunately, they are responsible for bringing the liquor and have to rely on a friend with a fake ID in the name of "McLovin."

Tenacious D in The Pick of Destiny (2006) R

Jack Black and Kyle Gass, who make up the real life rock band Tenacious D, must win a contest at a bar and decide that the only way to do so is to get a magical guitar pick.

That Thing You Do! (1996) PG

A one hit wonder band called The Wonders rises out of Erie, Pennsylvania in 1964 to hit the big time, only to fall.

Time Bandits (1981) PG United Kingdom

Kevin, a young boy in 1981 England, discovers that he has a time hole in his closet when a knight in armor jumps a horse over his bed. Kevin next discovers in his room a band of Little People who have a strange stolen map and soon the adventure of a lifetime begins.

The Wackness (2008) R

New high school graduate Luke sells marijuana, exchanges some for therapy sessions with Dr. Squires, and falls for Squire's step-daughter in this comedy that won the Audience Award at the 2008 Sundance Film Festival. Set on the west side of New York City in 1994.

Wayne's World (1992) PG-13
Wayne's World 2 (1993) PG-13

Mike Myers and Dana Carvey transport their famous *Saturday Night Live* characters to the movies. Wayne and his friend Garth live in Aurora, Illinois where they run a cable television show out of Wayne's parents' basement.

Weird Science (1985) PG-13

Two high school geeks find out that being with a woman means they have to become men after they create the perfect woman in this John Hughes film.

What a Girl Wants (2003) PG

In this comedy, an American teen goes to live with her very proper, upper crust father in England and does her best to fit in.

Whatever It Takes (2000) PG-13

Teen film adaptation of the Cyrano de Bergerac story. Ryan seeks to win Ashley's heart with Chris's help, but only if Ryan can help Chris gets close to Ryan's friend Maggie. A cute, if weak, romantic comedy.

White Chicks (2004) PG-13

The Wayans brothers are African American FBI agents who go under-cover in an all-white sorority house.

Whiteboyz (1999) R

Flip and his two friends live in Iowa, and want nothing more than to be like their rapper heroes, Dr. Dre and Snoop Dogg. But when they move to Chicago, things are not what they expected.

You Don't Mess With the Zohan (2008) PG-13

An ex-Mossad soldier, played by Adam Sandler, fakes his own death to come to America and become a hair stylist.

6

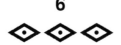

EDUCATION AND THE ARTS: SUGGESTED FILMS

According to the Kaiser Family Foundation Study "Generation M: Media in the Lives of 8–18 Year-olds," 46 percent of all 8- to 18-year-olds read a book on a typical day. However, according to that same study, 47 percent of children in the same age group play video games on a typical day, while 39 percent watch television or films. In other words, teens spend as much time watching television, watching films, and playing video games as they do reading books. In light of the results of this study, it is critical that young adult librarians begin recognizing the importance of these alternative media, assessing their respective impacts on teenagers, and building appropriate collections to keep teen patrons returning to the libraries.

Building a teen film collection means gathering independent, foreign, classic, documentary, and contemporary films that appeal directly to the target age group. However, films in the collection can also reach the intended audience *indirectly* through use by teachers, professors, and other instructors. Now that films are so varied and accessible, including them in a classroom setting can have an extraordinary effect on standard lesson planning—and, as a result, an extraordinary effect on the students themselves. Many books, short stories, plays, and graphic novels have been adapted for film, while documentary films and films about the performing arts provide insight into real life people and situations. Additionally, utilizing films in the classroom can provide support for students a different learning styles, or for those who suffer difficulties with traditional teaching methods.

Having a film collection for teens gives you the opportunity to include old classic films (the 1962 film *To Kill a Mockingbird*), newer classic films (the 1985 film *The Breakfast Club*), cult films (the 1975 film *The Rocky Horror Picture Show*), as well as other films that are obscure and not usually found in library film collections at all (the 2003 film *Noi*). Some of these obscure films would undoubtedly be foreign films that prior to this time were not readily available for acquisition; this is essential, as many films currently popular with teens fall into the independent and foreign categories. For example, young adults have made Japanese anime so popular and widely watched that it is now considered mainstream. A teen video collection without anime features would therefore be considered incomplete. Films constitute visual storytelling, so it is just as important for libraries to own and promote a teen video collection as it is for them to own and promote a teen book collection.

FILMED SHAKESPEARE

A solid teen film collection contains more than mass market films; for example, so many of the Shakespeare plays have been filmed in such a variety of ways (such as the 2002 film *A Midsummer Night's Rave)* that a class might watch three different and unique versions of the same play right in their own classroom.

While it would be impossible to list all of the many films that could be used effectively in the classroom, Shakespeare is a fairly universal topic of study. Many directors have tried to put their own imprint on a Shakespeare play, and British actor and director Kenneth Branagh is working his way through Shakespeare's canon and creating very entertaining updated versions. Some of the following modern film versions are perfect for teen audiences:

10 Things I Hate About You (1999) PG-13

> In this version of Shakespeare's *The Taming of the Shrew*, which is set in a Seattle high school, the potential suitors of popular Bianca Stafford hire a fellow student to take her unpopular older sister Kate to the prom so that Bianca can also attend.

As You Like It (2007) PG

> Kenneth Branagh sets Shakespeare's pastoral comedy in 19th-century Japan while his characters remain firmly English.

The Banquet [Original title: *Ye Yan*] (2006) NR

> Set in 10th-century China, this is a very loose, visually opulent adaptation of *Hamlet* by director Feng Xiaogang in the tradition of other contemporary Chinese epic films.

China Girl (1987) R

> Italian-American Tony meets Chinese-American Tian in this version of *Romeo and Juliet* as set in New York City during the 1980s.

The Complete Works of William Shakespeare (Abridged) (2000) NR
> Made for television

> Thirty-seven of Shakespeare's plays presented in under 90 minutes in a hilarious performance by Adam Long, Reed Martin, and Austin Tichenor, who make up The Reduced Shakespeare Company.

Hamlet (1996) PG-13

> Kenneth Branagh directs and stars in this four-hour *Hamlet* that features notable British actors, many of them famous Hamlets of the past, plus a delightful cameo performance by Billy Crystal as the Gravedigger.

Hamlet (2000) R

> Ethan Hawke's Hamlet is the young heir to the Denmark Corporation in contemporary New York City.

Hamlet (1991) PG

> Mel Gibson gives a first-rate performance as Hamlet. Director Franco Zeffirelli's film makes the complicated plot accessible to teen audiences.

Hamlet 2 (2008) R

> At Mesa High School in Tucson, Arizona, a high school teacher puts on a crazy sequel to *Hamlet*, complete with a musical number called "Rock Me Sexy Jesus."

Henry V (1989) PG-13

> Kenneth Branagh stars and directs this thrilling version of a young king's ascent to leadership.

The Hobart Shakespeareans (2005) NR Documentary

> Real life Los Angeles teacher Rafe Esquith helps his inner city fifth-grade students stage *Hamlet* with help from classroom visitors Michael York and Sir Ian McKellan.

Kiss Me Kate (2003) NR

> This wonderful filmed Broadway revival of Cole Porter's classic musical based on Shakespeare's *The Taming of the* Shrew might be interesting to fans of *10 Things I Hate About You*.

Love's Labor's Lost (2000) PG

> Director Kenneth Branagh sets his offbeat version of Shakespeare's romantic comedy, complete with singing and dancing, on the eve of World War II.

Macbeth (2006) NR Australia

This raw and violent adaptation of *Macbeth* is set among criminal gangs in contemporary Melbourne, Australia.

A Midsummer Night's Dream (1935) NR

Despite its age, this black-and-white movie version still resonates with viewers.

A Midsummer Night's Dream (1999) PG-13

An international cast of well-known actors brighten this delightful version of the play. Set in 19th-century Italy.

A Midsummer Night's Rave (2002) R

Teens may appreciate this loose adaptation of *A Midsummer Night's Dream* set in a rave in the woods outside Los Angeles, California.

Much Ado About Nothing (1993) PG-13

Director Kenneth Branagh assembles an all-star cast for this Shakespearean story of matchmaking, courtship, and jealous intrigue in a mythical villa in Italy.

O (2001) R

The story of *Othello* is relocated to a white boarding school in the American South, where the only African American student is basketball star Oden, whose love for Desi is subverted by fellow student Hugo.

Prince of the Himalayas (2006) NR China

Director Sherwood Hu's adaptation of *Hamlet* is set in ancient Tibet and performed in the Tibetan language.

Ran (1985) R Japan

Famed Japanese director Akira Kurosawa's epic masterpiece *Ran* is his interpretation of Shakespeare's *King Lear* as a 16th-century Japanese warlord.

Romeo + Juliet (1996) PG-13

Director Baz Luhrmann's retelling of *Romeo and Juliet* is set in the fictional Southern California city of Verona Beach. Starring Leonardo DiCaprio and Claire Danes, this film is extremely popular with teens.

Rosencrantz and Guildenstern are Dead (1991) PG

This filmed version of playwright Tom Stoppard's play of the same name is the story of two minor characters from *Hamlet* trying to understand the play going on around them and why they have to die.

Scotland, Pa. (2001) R

In this dark and funny satire, Mr. and Mrs. Macbeth work in a fast food restaurant for store manager Norm Duncan in 1970s Pennsylvania.

She's the Man (2006) PG-13

In this contemporary version of *Twelfth Night*, Viola dresses like her fraternal twin brother so she can take his place playing soccer for Illyria Prep School.

Shakespeare Behind Bars (2005) NR Documentary

Inmates of the Luther Luckett Correctional Complex in Kentucky stage *The Tempest*.

Shakespeare in Love (2004) R

While writing *Romeo and Juliet*, the up-and-coming Shakespeare meets a noblewoman with a desire to perform on the stage, something that's illegal in 16th-century England.

Shakespeare Retold (2005) NR

Technically a television series from the British Broadcasting Corporation, *Shakespeare Retold* is four modern retellings of *Much Ado About Nothing*, *Macbeth*, *The Taming of the Shrew*, and *A Midsummer Night's Dream*.

Stage Beauty (2005) R

Set during a production of Shakespeare's *Othello*, *Stage Beauty* is the story of a female actor who takes on the part of Desdemona after Charles II changed the law that barred actresses from the stage, setting off crises for a male actor who has always played the part.

Street King [Alternate title: *King Rikki*] (2002) R

Set in the barrio of East Los Angeles, this raw retelling of Shakespeare's *Richard III* follows Rikki as he betrays his family and friends in his quest for power.

Twelfth Night: Or What You Will (1996) PG

Director Trevor Nunn's version is distinguished by the fine performance of Imogen Stubbs as the female-disguised-as-male Viola in this love story of disguises and misunderstandings.

Valley Girl (1983) R

Director Martha Coolidge's version of *Romeo and Juliet* set in 1980s Los Angeles is the story of Valley Girl Julie falling for Randy, a Hollywood punk.

Were the World Mine (2008) NR

Director Tom Gustafson's independent film is set in an all-male prep school where students are putting on *A Midsummer Night's Dream*. After gay outcast Timothy, who has a crush jock Jonathan, is cast as Puck, he finds a real love potion that causes people to fall in love with the first person they see. Gustafson based this feature length film on his own short film entitled *Fairies*.

West Side Story (1961) NR

Perhaps one of the best-known retellings of *Romeo and Juliet* and winner of 10 Academy Awards, *West Side Story* is set in a New York City neighborhood in the 1960s. Some teens find it dated, but Leonard Bernstein's extraordinary music hooks other teens.

Many of the films referenced in this book are rated PG-13 or R, and as such may present a problem being screened in public schools. Even if that's the case, educators should still be able to use specific scenes from films in order to demonstrate a point or initiate a dialogue. For example, a teacher might supplement a discussion of women's roles in 16th- and 17th-century drama with appropriate clips from the 2004 R-rated film *Stage Beauty*, a film about the rise of female stage actors and their gradual replacement of the male stage actors traditionally cast in female roles. Furthermore, clips demonstrating how male actors originally portrayed females on stage could be pulled from films such as the 1998 R rated film *Shakespeare in Love*. This film offers the added benefit of showing the interactions between the stage players and the audience in the theaters of Shakespeare's time.

DOCUMENTARIES AND DOCUDRAMAS

Another way to utilize films in the classroom is to show docudramas such as those that take historical events and put them into a human context. For example, the 1995 made-for-television film *The Tuskegee Airmen* demonstrates how a fictional film or docudrama can bring history to life, particularly the history that is left out of the textbooks. What *The Tuskegee Airmen* did for African American WWII fighter pilots, similar films have done for the Navajo code talkers, civil rights proponents, union activists, and a wide array of other subjects and people.

Some of the best films with educational value are documentaries, so it is fortunate for librarians and young adults alike that, at the time of writing, we are in what seems to be the Golden Age of Documentaries. Traditionally, documentaries have been considered off the professional filmmaking and distributing grid; these films were typically produced on small budgets by educational institutions, then financed through grants or private organizations. For example, the film that most film historians cite as the first documentary, Robert Flaherty's 1922 film *Nanook of the North*, was funded by the French fur company Revillon Freres. It was also not uncommon for independent filmmakers to fund their own documentaries and secure screenings at local art theaters as a form of distribution.

Another avenue through which documentaries have been traditionally produced and distributed is public broadcasting organizations. For example, the National Film Board of Canada began producing excellent and award winning documentaries and short films when it was established in 1939 on the recommendation of John Grierson, a British documentary filmmaker. Likewise, when the National Educational Television (NET) network was created in the United States in 1952, it began to show documentaries on all manner of topics. In 1970, NET was replaced by the Public Broadcasting Service (PBS), and as such is still a major venue for documentaries; for example, PBS's *In The Mix* initiative, conceived in 1992, continues to focus specifically on documentaries based on subjects of interest to young people.

The increased visibility and influence of major film screening events like the Cannes Film Festival, the Sundance Film Festival, and the Edinburgh International Film Festival helps documentary filmmakers reach potential viewers. They also publicize unknown documentary film makers to attendees already well established in the industry.

Until recently, documentaries remained largely independent of the mass market film making business. In 1989, Michael Moore released his feature length film *Roger & Me*, the tragic story of a series of massive lay-offs and plant closures by General Motors in and around Moore's hometown of Flint, Michigan. The Roger referred to in the title is Roger Smith, who was the CEO of General Motors at the time of production. The film itself chronicles Moore's attempts to interview Smith about the financial decimation of Flint, and what responsibility General Motors, as the city's largest employer, bore towards its inhabitants. The film is funny, irreverent, manipulative, and even misleading, but it is nonetheless a riveting and timeless story. It is the story of Common Man versus the Corporation, who wins the battle in this film and continues to win the war. With the release of this documentary, Moore succeeded in capturing a mass market audience and proved that similar films had a legitimate place in the motion picture industry; in other words, Moore proved that documentaries could be entertaining, and that they could make money. After the critical and financial success of *Roger & Me*, Moore went on to do a slew of other films. According to the Box Office Mojo Web site, his documentary *Fahrenheit 9/11* about the 2001 attacks on the World Trade Center grossed nearly $24 million during its theatrical run and an estimated $120 million in total. Moore's 2007 exploration of the American healthcare system, *Sicko*, has already earned over $24 million at the time of writing.

Following in Michael Moore's footsteps and attempting to gear a documentary towards a broader audience, filmmaker Morgan Spurlock created another blockbuster with the 2004 film *Super Size Me*. In this film, Spurlock chronicles his experiences eating nothing but food from McDonald's restaurants for 30 days; over the course of the film he discovers that apart from gaining weight, his body begins to medically decline at a rapid speed. With the surprising popularity of *Super Size Me*, the subject of fast food restaurants came to the forefront of the American psyche and stayed controversial for some time. In 2006, director Richard Linklater produced a fictional film *Fast Food Nation*, based on the 2001 nonfiction bestseller

Fast Food Nation: The Dark Side of the All American Meal by Eric Schlosser. Filmmakers found inspiration for fiction films from true events. Many of the sports films listed in this guide are based on documentaries. In 2005, *The March of the Penguins* grossed $77 million, and, as film critic Robert Ebert pointed out, made more money than any of the five films nominated by the Academy Awards committee for Best Picture that year. Be aware when purchasing this film that the American version of *The March of the Penguins* is narrated, while the original French version has the penguins speaking to one another. Another nature film that did well financially was *Winged Migration*. Ecological documentaries *An Inconvenient Truth* and *The 11th Hour*, both released in 2007, not only got wide theatrical releases— perhaps due to the celebrities connected with them—but also did quite well both financially and critically.

Another benefit of documentaries, in addition to their more traditional use as educational or instructional tools, is that they are the kind of films that can serve as primers for teen filmmakers. Often the stories are intimate and personal, so they lend themselves well to a less practiced director, photographer, editor, or sound recorder. As such, documentaries have become extremely popular with the teen patrons at the authors' library in the past few years.

Whether by making them or watching them, documentaries are a great way to expose teens to the human condition and the state of the world, while at the same time initiating a discussion on the nature of truth. The following documentaries are likely to amuse, anger, agitate, or appall, but once viewed they will not easily be forgotten. For a generation that spends a large amount of its time in cyberspace, watching television, viewing films, and playing video games, a dose of reality may hit hard. Even more importantly, these current documentaries may create a sensibility and sensitivity in a new generation that must live with the world it inherits.

It should be noted, however, that documentaries as a format are usually first person narratives and can be highly prejudiced and one sided, even when they attempt to be objective and present both sides of a story.

What to Look for When Selecting

- Look for films that have received awards from film festivals. Many documentaries still make their debuts at national and international film festivals.
- The Academy of Motion Picture Arts and Sciences has been honoring Feature Documentary films with Academy Awards since 1942.

The award for Best Feature Documentary has been controversial in the past and remains so despite recently revised rules.

- Discover what films are being aired on cable television channels like the Sundance Channel and the Independent Film Channel, as the films aired on cable channels may lead to patron requests or suggestions for titles to include in your collection.

- Documentaries that appeal to teens may be about topics that might surprise selectors, such as global warming and the food industry. Films that are popular and interesting to adults can also be popular with teens, so keep an open mind.

Documentaries and Docudramas

5 Girls (2001) NR

From the PBS *POV (Point of View)* series, this fine film chronicles two years in the lives of five girls, ages 13 to 17.

The 11th Hour (2007) PG

Leonardo DiCaprio co-produced and narrated this look at the global environment.

Autism: the Musical (2007) NR

The Miracle Project gathered a group of autistic kids and adult caregivers together to put on a musical. Watching these children struggle to perform is affecting, powerful, and heartrending.

Bigger, Stronger, Faster (2008) NR

Director Christopher Bell examines his own steroid use as well as that of his two brothers in the context of the American drive to be the best.

Bowling for Columbine (2002) R

Michael Moore takes on the culture of fear in America in light of the Columbine school shootings.

Breaking the Silence (2003) NR

This video from the National Center for Lesbian Rights presents the stories of 10 young people raised in foster care who identified themselves as lesbian, gay, bisexual, transgender, or queer (LGBTQ).

The Conscientious Objector (2004) NR

The story of Desmond T. Doss, who won the Congressional Medal of Honor for his heroism as a medic during World War II despite the fact that he never touched a weapon.

Country Boys (2005) NR

This documentary, which originally aired on PBS's *Frontline* television series, follows three years in the lives of two Kentucky teens, Cody and Chris.

Deadline (2004) NR

> Filmmakers Katy Chevigny and Kirsten Johnson show how a class of journalism students caused the governor of Illinois, George Ryan, to commute the sentences of prisoners on death row.

The Education of Shelby Knox: Sex, Lies & Education (2004) NR

> Shelby Knox is a teen in the Lubbock, Texas school system who takes on the Board of Education to try to get a realistic sex education curriculum in her school, which is beset with high rates of teen pregnancies and sexually transmitted diseases. From the PBS *POV (Point of View)* series.

Emmanuel's Gift (2005) G

> When crippled teen Emmanuel Ofosu Yeboah receives a prosthetic leg, he journeys across his native Ghana on a bike to enlighten his countrymen about the plight of his fellow handicapped, and, therefore, socially ostracized people.

Fahrenheit 9/11 (2004) R

> Michael Moore's award-winning film on how President Bush and his administration handled events following the bombings in the United States after September 11.

The Fog of War: Eleven Lessons from the Life of Robert S. McNamara (2003) PG-13

> Robert S. McNamara, former Secretary of Defense who served during the Vietnam War, discusses what he thinks should have been done differently. It is a fascinating conversation.

The Future of Food (2004) NR

> *The Future of Food* is director Deborah Koons Garcia's film about the systematic destruction of the family-owned and run farm by big business and the push for genetically modified and engineered food.

Grizzly Man (2005) R

> Werner Herzog's award-winning film tells the story of Timothy Treadwell, who, in 1990, went to live and protect the grizzly bears in Alaska until he and his girlfriend were killed by their beloved bears in 2003.

An Inconvenient Truth (2006) PG

> Vice President Al Gore brought the disturbing facts of global warming to the American public and, even more importantly, to the citizens of the world.

Jesus Camp (2006) PG-13

> *Jesus Camp* is an inside look at Kids On Fire, a children's summer camp run by evangelical Christians in North Dakota.

The King of Kong (2007) PG-13

> When Billy Mitchell, holder of the highest score in the arcade game *Donkey Kong* for 25 years is beaten by Steve Weibe, they face each other in order to win a place in the Guinness Book of World Records.

The March of the Penguins (2005) G United States

> The dialogue of the original version of this film was replaced by narration by Morgan Freeman, which gave more biological facts about penguin behavior.

La Marche de L'Empereur (2005) NR

> When Director Jacques Perrin's film premiered at the Sundance Film Festival, the penguins talked to each other to communicate the reasons for their behavior.

Maya Lin: A Strong Clear Vision (2003) NR

> Maya Lin was a 21-year-old Yale architecture student when her design for the Vietnam Veterans Memorial won out of over 1000 designs submitted.

Mighty Times: The Children's March (2004) NR

> On May 2, 1963, the children of Birmingham, Alabama marched to protest segregation, facing fire hoses and police dogs. This Oscar winning, 40-minute-long documentary by Robert Houston won the Academy Award in 2005.

The Perfect Life: Growing Up in Urban America (2007) NR

> Englishwoman Sam Lee went to America in 1992 and taught second grade in a Harlem school aimed at disadvantaged children. Ten years later she went back to see how they were faring.

Rivers and Tides: Working With Time (2001) NR

> This award-winning documentary on the artistic creations of Scottish artist Andy Goldsworthy is breathtaking, not only in the photography but in the sheer joy in nature of the artist's work.

Roger & Me (1989) R

> Filmmaker Michael Moore's first documentary about the plight of the American working class forever revolutionized the film industry by becoming a box office hit.

Slippin': Ten Years with the Bloods (2005) NR

> Filmmakers Joachim and Tommy Sowards 10-year-long look at the gang life of the Bloods of Los Angeles.

Sicko (2007) PG-13

> Veteran documentary maker and long time malcontent Michael Moore takes on the American healthcare industry.

Sir! No Sir! (2005) NR

> *Sir! No Sir!* is a riveting documentary about the soldiers and veterans of the Vietnam War who became part of the antiwar movement of the 60s and 70s, both in and out of the armed forces.

Spellbound (2003) G

> *Spellbound* tells the story of 8 children between the ages of 8 and 14 as they compete in the 1999 Scripps-Howard National Spelling Bee in Washington, D.C.

Super Size Me (2004) PG-13

>   *Super Size Me* is Morgan Spurlock's disturbing film about the health consequences of living on McDonald's food for 30 days.

Thin (2006) NR Documentary

>   Director Lauren Greenfield spent six months at the Renfrew Center interviewing and filming four young women aged 15 to 30 battling eating disorders; they are fighting for their very lives.

Tupac: Resurrection (2003) R

>   Successful Gangsta Rap artist Tupac Shakur was a poet, philosopher, songwriter, and singer. Lauren Lazin's documentary reveals, often in Tupac's own words, the rise and early death at age 25 of a talented and thoughtful, but perhaps misguided, man.

The Trials of Darryl Hunt (2006) PG-13

>   Filmmakers Ricki Stern and Annie Sunderland's powerful indictment of the racial bias of the American justice system chronicles the wrongful imprisonment of Darryl Hunt and his 20-year quest to for freedom.

War Dance (2008) PG-13

>   Three children, the victims of war and violence, are invited to participate in a music festival in the capital city of their native Uganda. Nominated for an Academy Award, Best Documentary Feature in 2007.

We Are Wizards (2008) NR

>   Filmmaker Josh Koury's look at obsessed fans and critics of the Harry Potter books and movies.

What the Bleep Do We Know? (2004) NR

>   In a mix of New Age documentary and framing story, Marlee Matlin plays photographer Amanda in this unique attempt to explain quantum physic using graphics, talking head science experts, and a 35,000-year-old mystic Ramtha, as channeled by a woman named JZ Knight.

When the Levees Broke: A Requiem in Four Acts (2006) NR

>   Director Spike Lee's extraordinary film on the aftermath of Hurricane Katrina, which devastated New Orleans in 2005. With archival footage, superb use of music, and the heartbreaking stories of the survivors, Lee has created a masterpiece.

Winged Migration [original title: *Le Peuple migrateur*] (2002) G France, Spain, Italy, Germany, and Switzerland.

>   Director Jacques Perrin's Oscar Nominated film follows migratory birds across all seven continents. More than 450 people, including 14 cinematographers, took three years to create this amazing film.

Who Killed the Electric Car? (2006) PG

>   In 1990, the California Air Resources Board adopted the Zero Emission Vehicle mandate, which required that 2 percent of cars in the state be in compliance by 1998. Why this didn't happen is every bit as intriguing as any suspense story.

The Wild Parrots of Telegraph Hill (2003) G

> Mark Bittner, a homeless musician in San Francisco, cares for one of the city's wild parrot flocks. More than the fascinating story of what Mark learns about the parrots is the story of Mark himself, and what happens when he has to say goodbye to his birds.

Wordplay (2006) PG

> The surprising and delightful story of crossword puzzles: who makes them, how they are made, and who solves them.

PERFORMING ARTS FILMS

Music performances, dance concerts, and musical theater lend themselves to being filmed. Plays can become vital and lively when seen on the screen and are much more interesting than their printed counterparts. Music is overwhelmingly important to teens. Since the birth of rock and roll, teens have come to define themselves by their music, regardless of what another generation thinks. Today's teens carry iPods or MP3 players with hundreds if not thousands of songs on them. When the MTV music television channel was launched in 1981 to play music videos, it transformed the music business. Music now has a visual aspect to it. Seeing the success of MTV, the film industry was quick to realize the potential of marrying popular music with films. Music is so much a part of the finished product of a movie that owning soundtracks of the films in your teen collection is highly recommended and will undoubtedly prove popular with patrons.

What to Look for When Selecting

- Any musical or play that the local middle or high school is planning on presenting or has ever presented.
- Filmed concerts of musicians and bands that are popular with your teens. Note that most of these are not rated and may contain bad language, drug references, and nudity.
- Look for musicals created for television and cable.
- Consider a sampling of ballet and contemporary dance films to test your teen patrons' tastes

Filmed Performing Arts Performances

Across the Universe (2007) PG-13

> A Liverpool longshoreman travels to New York, meets a girl named Lucy, and the pair go on a journey of discovery and exploration of pop cul-

ture during the 1960s and 1970s, accompanied by music from the Beatles. Fabulous.

Air Guitar Nation (2005) R Documentary

Air Guitar Nation is a hilarious film about the first two American contestants in the 2003 World Air Guitar Championship in Oulu, Finland.

Amandla: A Revolution in Four Part Harmony (2002) PG-13 Documentary

This film documents the history and background of the role that music played in keeping the goal of freedom alive during apartheid in South Africa. A powerful and unforgettable documentary.

The American Mall (2008) NR Made for television

MTV's version of the wildly successful Disney Channel movie *High School Musical*, is set at a mall where talented teen Aly loves music and the equally talented Joey.

Andrew Lloyd Webber's The Phantom of the Opera (2004) PG-13

With dazzling set designs, elaborate costumes, and glorious singing, this is a great film version of Lloyd Webber's hit musical. Based on Gaston Leroux's novel of the same name, this is the story of a disfigured musical madman who haunts the Paris Opera and falls in love with a young and talented opera singer.

Antonia (2007) PG-13

Four young women form an all-female rap group to escape the poverty of their lives in Sao Paulo, Brazil. *Antonia* documents their struggle to survive and eventually thrive in the end.

Awesome: I . . . Shot That (2006) R

While performing a concert in Madison Square Garden in 2004, the Beastie Boys distributed 50 cameras to fans to film the concert and created a very unique concert video.

Blast! (2001) NR

Originally aired on the Public Broadcasting System and featuring brass, percussion, and visual performers, *Blast!* is a tribute to the uniquely American musical entertainment, the football half-time show.

Camp (2003) PG-13

Theatrically inclined teens spend the summer at Camp Ovation, where they flirt, fight, sing, and dance. As in the film *Fame*, these kids love doing what they do at a place where they fit in.

Camp Rock (2008) NR

Created by the producers of the hit TV series *High School Musical, Camp Rock* follows a group of teenagers who go to summer camp.

Carmen: A Hip Hopera (2001) PG-13

MTV's movie take on Bizet's *Carmen* starring Beyonce is watchable, but doesn't quite come off. Still, this film succeeds as an introduction to opera for teens.

Cats (1998) NR

This is a filmed performance of Andrew Lloyd Webber's hit musical, which is based on T.S. Eliot's book of poetry, *Old Possum's Book of Practical Cats* and features actors singing and dancing as cats.

Center Stage (2000) PG-13
Center Stage: Turn It Up (2008) PG-13

The *Center Stage* films are the fictional stories of a group of young people as they spend their first and second years at the American Ballet Center.

Criss Angel, Mindfreak: Halloween Special (2005) NR

From Arts and Entertainment Home Video, this is a taped special performance of the famous street magician, who is very popular with teens.

Cry-Baby (1990) PG-13

John Water's homage to teen films of the 1950s takes place in 1954 Baltimore where Cry-Baby, a juvenile delinquent, is loved by the Good Girl Allison. Like *Hairspray*, *Cry-Baby* has been made into a musical.

Dirty Dancing (1987) PG-13
Dirty Dancing: Havana Nights (2004) PG-13

An idealistic, thoughtful young girl starts dancing with the young man her adoring father would object to the most. These are great teen films for a variety of reasons.

Drumline (2002) PG-13

A talented teen drummer from Harlem wins a scholarship to an Atlanta university, and must learn to be part of the band and not a solo act.

El Cantante (2007) R

El Cantante, which is Spanish for "The Singer", is the story of Hector Lavoe, a native Puerto Rican who came to New York in 1963 and revolutionized the Latin music world with Salsa. Marc Anthony as Lavoe and Jennifer Lopez as Lavoe's wife will attract teen viewers.

Fame (1980) R

Fairly grim and edgy by today's standards, this was a breakout film when it premiered and paved the way for the teen musical movies of today. It's the story of the students at New York City High School for the Performing Arts over a four-year period.

The Fighting Temptations (2004) PG

An out of work New Yorker is left $150,000 by his aunt, but only if he can lead his old small town Georgia church choir to victory in the Gospel Explosion competition.

Footloose (1984) PG

When an urban teen moves to a rural town, he can't believe that the town elders and with the minster have forbidden dancing within the town limits, so he sets out to reinstate prom night.

Godspell: A Musical Based on the Gospel According to Saint Matthew (1973) G

> The film version of this joyful and lively stage musical has Jesus and His disciples dressed as street performers and hippies in a modern urban landscape.

Grease (1978) PG
Grease 2 (1982) PG

> The first of these films about high school life in 1950s America is in the list of the top grossing films ever made, and is, for a lot of libraries, the top circulating title. A classic, it experienced a revival when it was staged on Broadway. The sequel has become a kind of cult classic with its own set of fans.

Hair (1979) PG

> During the Vietnam War, a young man from the Midwest gets drafted and meets hippies in New York City in this rock musical.

Hairspray (1988) PG
Hairspray (2007) PG

> An overweight girl who is a great dancer, Tracy Turnblad, tries to get on a local dance television program in 1960s Baltimore. The first movie is one of director John Waters best, and the second is the film version of the Tony Award winning Broadway musical.

High School Musical (2006) G Made for television
High School Musical 2 (2007) PG-13 Made for television
High School Musical 3: Senior Year (2008) PG

> In the first of these Disney Channel films, two high school students, a brain and a jock, decide to audition for the school musical and find that the experience changes them both. Sequels follow the same characters as they go through high school.

The History Boys (2006) R United Kingdom

> This extraordinary film adaptation of Alan Bennett's award winning play finds teachers and students in a boys' school in northern England in 1983 discussing the nature and importance of history in education.

House Party (1990) R

> Two middle class African American guys, Kid and Play, go to a free-for-all party in this wild and hip film. The sequels are not recommended.

Jailhouse Rock (1957) NR

> Juvenile delinquent Vince Everett, played by Elvis Presley, is sent to jail, where he learns about the music business from his cellmate. After his release from prison, he becomes a rock star. Classic rock movie with a classic rock star.

Joseph and the Amazing Technicolor Dreamcoat (1999) NR

> Andrew Lloyd Webber and Tim Rice create a rocking musical version of the Bible story.

The Last Waltz (1978) PG

At the center of this rock documentary, directed by Martin Scorsese, is the farewell concert of The Band after 16 years together.

Mad Hot Ballroom (2005) PG Documentary

Mad Hot Ballroom is a fascinating and heart warming documentary about three different schools in New York that participate in the city's ballroom dancing competition.

Mamma Mia! (2008) PG-13

When Sophie becomes engaged to Sky, she discovers in her mother's diary the names of the three men who might possibly be her father. So she invites the three to the wedding, and the plot unfolds with singing and dancing all to the music of the pop group ABBA.

OT: Our Town (2003) NR Documentary

In Compton, California, the teachers at Dominguez High School choose to produce the reputedly most frequently performed play, Thornton Wilder's *Our Town*. What the students do with a play very far out of their ken makes an intriguing film.

Our Town (2005) NR

This film compilation consists of two historic versions of Thornton Wilder's masterpiece: a 1977 made-for-television production starring Hal Holbrook and a 1989 version starring Spalding Gray.

Rent (2005) PG-13

This is a great film version of Jonathan Larson's Tony and Pulitzer Prize winning musical play about eight friends dealing with life and death in New York City's East Village in 1996 as AIDS affects the community. For teens, this loose adaptation of *La Boheme* is one of the most popular musicals ever made.

Rize (2005) PG-13 Documentary

Rize is a documentary about "krumping" a kind of freestyle, improvised dancing done by performers sometimes dressed as clowns in parts of Los Angeles. Unbelievable dance performances and unforgettable characters.

Rocky Horror Picture Show (1975) R

A box office flop when it opened, this musical tells the story of what can happen to a couple of white middle class young adults when they meet an alien "sweet transvestite from Transsexual, Transylvania." A cult classic with out there cinematography and costumes recalling the '30s, '40s, and '50s.

Shine a Light (2008) PG-13

Martin Scorsese's film tribute to the iconic rock and roll band the Rolling Stones is a combination of the filming of a 2006 concert in New York interspersed with archival footage and commentary.

Saawarlya (2007) PG India

A beautiful woman meets a musician and they spend an enchanted evening together. Based on Dostoevsky's short story "White Nights."

Stagedoor (2005) NR Documentary

Stagedoor Manor in New York State's Catskills Mountains is a summer camp for kids who love Broadway over baseball, and each hope that they can become famous like alumni Zach Braff and Natalie Portman.

Step Up (2006) PG-13
Step Up 2 the Streets (2008) PG-13

Baltimore delinquent Tyler Gage finds himself doing community service work at the Maryland School of the Arts, where he becomes the perfect dance partner for a talented young ballerina. Both films are formulaic but charming.

Stomp Out Loud (1997) NR

This made-for-cable video, which showcases performances by the extraordinary dance troop *Stomp*, is exciting, revealing, and well worth seeing.

Stomp the Yard (2007) PG-1

A talented dancer, urban teen DJ is accepted into a prestigious black university and gets caught up in a freestyle step dancing rivalry between two fraternity houses. A solid plot that involves DJ's family and friends make this an above average dance film.

Sweeney Todd: The Demon Barber of Fleet Street (2007) R

With Johnny Depp as the murderous barber, this film of the Stephen Sondheim hit musical has a good deal of teen appeal.

Take the Lead (2006) PG-13

Based on the true story of dance instructor Pierre Dulaine, who teaches inner city kids classical ballroom dancing as well as how to respect themselves and each other. The documentary *Mad Hot Ballroom* inspired this uplifting film.

Trapped in the Closet: Chapters 1–22 (2007) R

R. Kelly's rhythm and blues hip hop opera represents a new direction for music videos. Available on DVD.

You Got Served (2004) PG-13

There's great dancing but not much plot in this popular film about two street dancing crews who challenge each other to a dance duel.

The Wiz (1978) G

This lively musical based on L. Frank Baum's *The Wizard of Oz* features an all African American cast. A young Michael Jackson plays the scarecrow and Diana Ross takes the role of a very mature but rousing Dorothy.

Woodstock (1970) R Documentary

Despite extensive nudity and drug use, this is a must-see film for its musical performances, especially Jimi Hendrix playing his version of "The Star Spangled Banner," the American national anthem.

Yellow Brick Road (2006) NR Documentary

> A stage production of *The Wizard of Oz* is put on by the residents of a home for the mentally and physically challenged.

Zoot Suit (1981) NR

> Filmed version of the Broadway hit, this groundbreaking musical is set in the 1940s in the barrios of Los Angeles and is based on historical events.

FILMS MADE FROM BOOKS

In recent years, a great many teen novels have been adapted into films, which is great news for librarians for several reasons. When such novels generate box office successes, books aimed at teen audiences earn respect as sources for new films for filmmakers. This attention from filmmakers for teen novels has shown authors that writing books for teens can be as financially rewarding as writing adult books, and more publishers are willing to publish them. The impact these trends have upon libraries is dual fold. First, teens come into the library upon a book's initial release; second, when a film adaptation is released later on, the book becomes popular again and draws in new or returning readers.

Discussion groups on these popular book and film combinations are good places for teen fans to find other fans to talk with about what draws them to the works. Film discussion groups have many young adult titles to choose from, but there are some less obvious choices that may be very successful in a "Books to Film" type discussion group.

The titles listed below are only suggestions for getting started. Articles and books devoted to listing films on books are published regularly. Many library Web sites include lists on the topic and two, Teenreads.com and Educational Media Reviews Online, are covered in our chapter on reviews and resources. Most librarians can identify such book and film combinations within their collections.

Films set in the future are very popular with teens, as speculation about what is to come is especially interesting at that age. While adults might see a version of a dystopian world as horrifying, teens seem more comfortable with the idea of a world where machines do so much and hold such power. Though it sometimes seems that teens rarely read science fiction anymore, they are nonetheless often familiar with classic science fiction stories due to their popular film adaptations. For example, many of science fiction author Philip K. Dick's works have been made into successful films, including *Blade Runner* (1982), *Minority Report* (2002), *A Scanner Darkly* (2006), and *Radio Free Albemuth* (2008). Polish science fiction writer Stanislaw Lem saw his novel *Solaris* made into a popular 2002 film of the same name. Further successful films adapted from works by science fiction Grand Masters include Ray Bradbury's *Fahrenheit 451* (1966); Arthur C. Clarke's *2001: A Space Odyssey* (1968) and *2010* (1984); and Isaac Asimov's *Bicentennial Man* (1999) and *I, Robot* (2004).

Modern special effects allow filmmakers to create alien worlds and give their characters any skills or powers they can think up. Older science fiction films often remain viable precisely because of their strong sense of otherworldliness. Of course, the ultimate science fiction films constitute the wildly popular *Star Wars* series, a series more about the mythic hero's quest than about a future dictated by science and technology. These stories, which began as films and were later turned into books, have generated hundreds of science fiction books that are still very popular with teens.

Recent fantasy film blockbusters like the *Harry Potter* series, *The Lord of the Rings* trilogy, and the film *Eragon* (2006) have proven extremely popular with teens. While the special effects are stunning and provide great entertainment, the underlying reason for the popularity of these films with teens is most likely their focus on the conflict between good and evil. The idea of a quest may not occur to teens on a conscious level, but they are on a quest to become adults and to learn the difference between right and wrong. Consequently, it is easy to see why teens often identify with the heroes in fantasy films, whether or not they are aware of the reasons why.

When discussing books that have been made into films, one film that presents many topics for inspiring dialogue is Richard Linklater's *Waking Life* (2001). In an animation *tour de force*, Wiley Wiggins, one of the actors from Linklater's film *Dazed and Confused* (1993), plays a wandering Everyman who has a series of conversations with all manner of people on such concepts as existence, freedom, and evolution. Teens love the surreal animation styles and appreciate the movie simply because it challenges them to think. Three other films that will undoubtedly inspire further discussion have been mentioned previously in this book: *Elephant* (2003), *Zero Day* (2003), and *Home Room* (2002). These films all deal with the shocking and tragic Columbine High School massacre, but do so in very different ways; they are very likely to generate many comments from teens about what it is to be a student today.

Offering film combinations, whether through programs or merely by recommendations on bookmarks, is a way to communicate to teens that some films are more than merely lightweight forms of entertainment or blips on the pop culture radar. Hollywood remakes old films all the time, and the remakes are not necessarily the better films. The future will bring more spectacular special effects, but also the probability that films will become even more important as a primary way to tell stories. Libraries need to recognize that films are as integral to the lives of current teens as are young adult novels. Both collections are critical for serving teen patrons.

30 Days of Night (2008) R

>Based on the graphic novels of Ben Templeton and Steve Niles.

300 (2006) R

>Based on the graphic novel of the same name by Frank Miller.

1408 (1983) PG-13

>Based on a short story of the same name by Stephen King.

1984 (1984) R United Kingdom

>Based on the novel of the same name by George Orwell.

The Adventures of Huckleberry Finn (1960) NR
Huckleberry Finn (1974) G
The Adventures of Huck Finn (1993) PG

>Based on the novel *Adventures of Huckleberry Finn* by Mark Twain.

All Quiet on the Western Front (1930) PG Black and white
All Quiet on the Western Front (1979) NR Made for television

>Based on the novel of the same name by Erich Maria Remarque.

Angela's Ashes (1999) R United States/Ireland

>Based on the novel of the same name by Frank McCourt.

Bartleby (2001) PG-13

>Based on the short story "Bartleby the Scrivener" by Herman Melville.

Beloved (1998) R

>Based on the novel of the same name by Toni Morrison.

Blade Runner (1982) R

>Based on the novel *Do Androids Dream of Electric Sheep?* by Philip K. Dick.

Blood and Chocolate (2007) PG-13

>Based on the novel of the same name by Annette Curtis Klause.

The Bourne Identity (2002) PG-13

>Based on the novels of the same name by Robert Ludlum.

Brokeback Mountain (2005) R

>Based on a short story by Annie Proulx.

Carrie (1976) R

> Based on the novel of the same name by Stephen King.

The Cider House Rules (1999) PG-13

> Based on the novel of the same name by John Irving.

The Chocolate War (1988) R

> Based on the novel of the same name by Robert Cormier.

The Chosen (1981) PG

> Based on the novel of the same name by Chaim Potok.

Christine (1983) R

> Based on the novel of the same name by Stephen King.

The Color Purple (1985) PG-13

> Based on the novel of the same name by Alice Walker.

Confessions of a Teenage Drama Queen (2004) PG

> Based on the novel of the same name by Dyan Sheldon.

The Count of Monte Cristo (2002) PG-13

> Based on the novel of the same name by Alexander Dumas.

The Crow (1994) R

> Based on the graphic novels of J. O'Barr.

A Cry in the Wild (1990) PG

> Based on the novel *Hatchet* by Gary Paulsen.

The Dead Poet's Society (1989) PG

> Based on the novel of the same name by N. H. Kleinbaum.

Dracula (1931) NR Black and white
Dracula (1992) R

> Based on the novel of the same name by Bram Stoker.

Drive Me Crazy (1999) PG-13

> Based on Todd Strasser's book, *How I Created My Perfect Prom Date*.

Dune (1984) PG-13

> Based on the novel of the same name by Frank Herbert.

Election (1999) R

> Based on the novel of the same name by Tom Perrotta.

Ella Enchanted (2004) PG

> Based on the novel of the same name by Gail Carson Levine.

Emma (1996) PG

> Based on the novel of the same name by Jane Austen.

The English Patient (1996) R

> Based on the novel of the same name by Michael Ondaatje.

Eragon (2006) PG

Based on the novel of the same name by Christopher Paolini.

Fahrenheit 451 (1996) NR United Kingdom

Based on the novel of the same name by Ray Bradbury.

Fear and Loathing In Las Vegas (1998) R

Based on the novel of the same name by Hunter S. Thompson.

Fight Club (1999) R

Based on the novel of the same name by Chuck Palahniuk.

The Five People You Meet in Heaven (2004) NR Made for television

Based on the book of the same name by Mitch Albom.

Freedom Writers (2007) PG-13

Based on the book *The Freedom Writers Diary* by Erin Gruwell.

Ghost World (2001) R

Based on the graphic novel of the same name by Daniel Clowes.

Girl, Interrupted (2000) R

Based on the book of the same name by Susanna Kaysen.

Gone with the Wind (1939) G

Based on the novel of the same name by Margaret Mitchell.

The Great Gatsby (1974) PG

Based on the novel of the same name by F. Scott Fitzgerald.

Harry Potter and the Sorcerer's Stone (2001) PG United Kingdom
Harry Potter and the Chamber of Secrets (2002) PG United Kingdom
Harry Potter and the Prisoner of Azkaban (2004) PG United Kingdom
Harry Potter and the Goblet of Fire (2005) PG-13 United Kingdom
Harry Potter and the Order of the Phoenix (2007) PG-13 United Kingdom
Harry Potter and the Half-Blood Prince (2009) PG-13 United Kingdom

Based on the novels of the same names by J. K. Rowling.

High Fidelity (2000) R

Based on the novel of the same name by Nick Hornby.

The Hitchhiker's Guide to the Galaxy (2005) PG

Based on the novel of the same name by Douglas Adams.

Holes (2003) PG

Based on the young adult novel of the same name by Louis Sachar.

Hoot (2006) PG

Based on the young adult novel of the same name by Carl Hiassen.

Howl's Moving Castle [alternate title *Hauru no ugoku shiro*] (2004) PG

Based on the novel of the same name by Diana Wynne Jones.

How to Deal (2003) PG-13

> Based on two of Sarah Dessen's novels combined: *Someone Like You* and *That Summer*.

How to Make an American Quilt (1995) PG-13

> Based on the novel of the same name by Whitney Otto.

I Am the Cheese (1983) PG

> Based on the young adult novel of the same name by Robert Cormier.

I Know What You Did Last Summer (1997) R

> Based on the young adult novel of the same name by Lois Duncan.

Jane Eyre (1944) NR Black and white
Jane Eyre (1996) PG United Kingdom

> Based on the novel of the same name by Charlotte Bronte.

The Joy Luck Club (1993) R

> Based on the novel of the same name by Amy Tan.

Killing Mr. Griffin (1997) PG-13

> Based on the young adult novel of the same name by Lois Duncan.

The Kite Runner (2007) PG-13

> Based on the novel of the same name by Khaled Hosseini.

The League of Extraordinary Gentlemen (2003) PG-13 United States/United Kingdom

> Based on the graphic novel of the same name by Alan Moore.

Little Women (1949) NR Black and white
Little Women (1994) PG

> Based on the novel of the same name by Louisa May Alcott.

Lord of the Flies (1963) NR United Kingdom
Lord of the Flies (1990) R

> Based on the novel of the same name by William Golding.

The Lord of the Rings: The Fellowship of the Ring (2001) PG-13 New Zealand/United States
The Lord of the Rings: The Two Towers (2002) PG-13 New Zealand/United States
The Lord of the Rings: The Return of the King (2003) PG-13 New Zealand/United States

> Based on the novels by J.R.R. Tolkien.

The Man in the Iron Mask (1998) PG-13

> Based on the novel of the same name by Alexander Dumas.

Mi Vida Loca (1993) R

> Based on the novel of the same name by Allison Anders.

Misery (1990) R

> Based on the novel of the same name by Stephen King.

Moby Dick (1930) NR Black and white

>   Based on the novel of the same name by Herman Melville.

The Neverending Story (1984) NR West Germany/United States

>   Based on the novel *Die Unendliche Geschichte* by Michael Ende.

Nick and Norah's Infinite Playlist (2008) PG-13

>   Based on the teen novel of the same name by Rachel Cohn and David Levithan.

Never Cry Wolf (1983) PG

>   Based on the novel of the same name by Farley Mowat.

The Mighty (1998) PG-13

>   Based on the young adult novel *Freak the Mighty* by Rodman Philbrick.

The Mist (2007) R

>   Based on the novella *The Mist* by Stephen King.

October Skies (1999) PG

>   Based on the book *Rocket Boys* by Homer H. Hickam, Jr.

Of Mice and Men (1992) PG-13

>   Based on the novel of the same name by John Steinbeck.

Oliver Twist (1948) NR United Kingdom Black and white
Oliver Twist (2005) PG-13 United Kingdom

>   Based on the novel of the same name by Charles Dickens.

One Flew Over the Cuckoo's Nest (1975) R

>   Based on the novel of the same name by Ken Kesey.

Ordinary People (1980) R

>   Based on the novel of the same name by Judith Guest.

The Outsiders (1983) PG-13

>   Based on the young adult novel of the same name by S. E. Hinton.

The Postman (1997) R

>   Based on the novel of the same name by David Brin.

Pride and Prejudice (1940) Approved
Pride and Prejudice (2005) PG United Kingdom

>   Based on the novel of the same name by Jane Austen.

The Princess Bride (1987) PG

>   Based on the novel of the same name by William Goldman.

The Princess Diaries (2001) G

>   Based on the novel of the same name by Meg Cabot. The sequel movie uses the characters but is not based on any known books.

The Puppet Masters (1994) R

>   Based on the novel of the same name by Robert A. Heinlein.

Rebecca (1940) NR Black and white

> Based on the novel of the same name by Daphne du Maurier.

The Red Badge of Courage (1951) NR
The Red Badge of Courage (1974) Made for television

> Based on the novel of the same name by Stephen Crane.

The Razor's Edge (1946) NR Black and white
The Razor's Edge (1984) PG-13

> Based on the novel of the same name by W. Somerset Maugham.

Road to Perdition (2002) R

> Based on the graphic novel of the same name by Max Allen Collins.

Robinson Crusoe (1997) PG-13

> Based on the novel *The Life and Adventures of Robinson Crusoe* by Daniel Defoe.

Rumble Fish (1983) R

> Based on the young adult novel of the same name by S. E. Hinton.

The Secret Life of Bees (2008) PG-13

> Based on the novel of the same name by Sue Monk Kidd.

Sense and Sensibility (1995) PG United States/United Kingdom

> Based on the novel of the same name by Jane Austen. There are a number of made for television versions available.

A Separate Peace (1972) PG
A Separate Peace (2004) R

> Based on the novel of the same name by John Knowles.

Shane (1953) Approved

> Based on the novel of the same name by Jack Schaefer.

The Shawshank Redemption (1994) R

> Based on the novella *Rita Hayworth and Shawshank Redemption* by Stephen King.

The Shining (1980) R

> Based on the novel of the same name by Stephen King.

Simon Birch (1998) PG

> Based on *A Prayer for Owen Meany* by John Irving.

Sin City (2005) R

> Based on the graphic novels by Frank Miller.

The Sisterhood of the Traveling Pants (2005) PG

> Based on the young adult novel of the same name by Ann Brashares.

The Sisterhood of the Traveling Pants 2 (2008) PG-13

> Based on the young adult novel *The Second Summer of the Sisterhood* by Ann Brashares.

Slaughterhouse-Five (1972) R

> Based on the novel *Slaughterhouse-Five Or The Children's Crusade* by Kurt Vonnegut.

Sleepy Hollow (1999) R

> Based the story *The Legend of Sleepy Hollow* by Washington Irving.

Stand By Me (1986) R

> Based on the short story *The Body* by Stephen King.

Starship Troopers (1997) R

> Based on the novel of the same name by Robert A. Heinlein.

Stormbreaker (2006) PG

> Based on the young adult novel of the same name by Anthony Horowitz.

A Tale of Two Cities (1935) NR Black and white
A Tale of Two Cities (1958) NR United Kingdom

> Based on the novel of the same name by Charles Dickens.

The Talented Mr. Ripley (1999) R

> Based on the novel of the same name by Patricia Highsmith.

Tex (1982) PG

> Based on the young adult novel of the same name by S. E. Hinton.

That Was Then...This Is Now (1985) R

> Based on the young adult novel of the same name by S. E. Hinton.

The Three Musketeers (1948) NR
The Three Musketeers (1993) PG

> Based on the novel of the same name by Alexandre Dumas.

The Time Machine 1960) G
The Time Machine (2002) PG-13

> Based on the novel of the same name by H. G. Wells.

To Kill a Mockingbird (1962) NR Black and white

> Based on the novel of the same name by Harper Lee.

Tom Sawyer (1973) G
Tom and Huck (1995) PG

> Based on the novel *The Adventures of Tom Sawyer* by Mark Twain.

Tuesdays With Morrie (1998) PG

> Based on the book of the same name by Mitch Albom.

V for Vendetta (2005) R

> Based on the graphic novel of the same name by Alan Moore.

The Virgin Suicides (1999) R

> Based on the novel of the same name by Jeffrey Eugenides.

What Dreams May Come (1998) PG-13

> Based on the novel of the same name by Richard Matheson.

When Zachary Beaver Came to Town (2005) PG

> Based on the young adult novel of the same name by Kimberly Willis Holt.

Where the Red Fern Grows (1974) G
Where the Red Fern Grows (2003) PG

> Based on the novel of the same name by Wilson Rawls.

The Yearling (1946) G
The Yearling (1994) NR

> Based on the novel of the same name by Marjorie Kinnan Rawlings.

7

FILM REVIEWS
AND RESOURCES

ONLINE VIDEO REVIEWS
AND REVIEW SOURCES

We have endeavored in this chapter to list the sites that have proven best for general reviews and also for film industry-related information. There are many, many other online professional movie review sites that we have not listed, as well as even more fan sites and blogs dedicated to film reviewing. Many of these unlisted choices can be effective and useful for your selection practices if you choose to investigate them.

Several of the online sources we've listed stand out from the crowd. Roger Ebert, nationally known critic for *The Chicago Sun-Times* newspaper, has consistently shown open-mindedness in his choice of films to review and an unusual insight in his reviews. He was among the first major film critics to review anime, and the range of films he has commented on is unique. *The New York Times* film reviews are also excellent and include many independent and foreign films not commonly found elsewhere. Lastly, if you only refer to one site, the Internet Movie Database is a huge and authoritative source for film information and provides access to film reviews you won't be able to track down elsewhere.

Anime News Network: http://www.animenewsnetwork.com

A comprehensive site begun in 1998 by Justin Sevakis; any important news and information on anime and manga will usually appear here first.

The DVD Journal: DVD News, Reviews, Commentary, and Stuff Like That: http://www.dvdjournal.com

This is a very helpful and informative site for any and all DVD-related topics and questions. The site offers the following: News & Commentary, Quick Reviews, Full Reviews, The Editor's Top 25, The Release Calendar, The Stat Sheet, The DVD Lexicon, Choice Web Links, and a particularly useful DVD MIA (Missing in Action) list of out of print DVDs and films never released in DVD format.

Educational Media Reviews Online: http://www.libweb.lib.buffalo.edu/emro

This excellent site provides information on a small collection of films, specifically offering critical descriptions of titles and how those titles can be used in an educational setting. This site often provides information found nowhere else that can prove useful for selectors.

The Internet Movie Database: http://www.imdb.com/

IMDb is one of the most extensive sites for finding all of the facts accumulated about a certain film. Born from a Usenet newsgroup called rec.arts.movies and manned by devoted video fans, IMDb was acquired by Amazon.com in 1998, which allowed the site to become the highly useful database that it is today. The search engine is excellent; a keyword search will bring up all of the films relevant to that word, followed by the year of release, which is helpful when there are films with the same name or when there are sequels. In addition to the keyword search, the site is searchable by titles, TV episode, names, production companies, characters, quotes, biographies, and plots. IMDb details information on both the theatrical and DVD releases of films and includes other categories of interest, including "Tops At The Box Office," "Opening This Week," "Coming Soon," "New DVDs this week," "New on Blu ray Hi DEF," "On TV Tonight," "User Favorites," and "Translated Sites."

Movie Review Query Engine: http://www.MRQE.com

This database contains print and online reviews for a huge number of film titles in an easy to use searchable format.

Gilles Poitras' Guides on Anime and Manga for selectors:

- Anime (and Manga) for Parents (and Other Grownups): www.koyagi.com/Parents
- Librarian's Guide to Anime and Manga: www.koyagi.com/Libguide.html
- Recommended Anime: www.koyagi.com/recAnime.html

Reel.com: http://www.reel.com

This site provides great short summaries and the site's own reviews. Particularly nice features include "Movie Match" and "Creative Movie

Match" categories that provide recommendations of films similar to a suggested title. A good place to look for help with "viewers advisory."

Roger Ebert.com: Movies and More: http://rogerebert.suntimes.com

For years, Roger Ebert has reviewed films generally considered outside the mainstream. He was also one of the first national critics to review anime.

Rotten Tomatoes: http://www.rottentomatoes.com

With nearly 250,000 titles in its database and more than three times as many reviews, Rotten Tomatoes is one of the best-known comprehensive review sites. It is searchable by title, person, plot, genre, MPAA ratings, era and decade, year, and critical reviews. The reviews are written by select "Approved Tomatometer Critics" who must meet exacting guidelines that can be found on the Web site.

Top Ten REVIEWS (Movie Review Section): http://www.movies.toptenreviews.com

The movie section of this site not only provides 10 reviews of each film but also contains lists of the best films of the decade and the year.

OTHER ONLINE FILM INFORMATION SOURCES

Boxoffice.com: http://www.boxoffice.com/

Boxoffice magazine began in 1920 and launched this site in 1994. Intended for industry professionals and theater owners, this site contains up-to-date information on the behind-the-scenes actions affecting films, including release dates, film grosses, casting, and distribution and production details.

Box Office Mojo: http://wwwboxofficemojo.com

Founded by Branson Gray in 1999, this site boasts the most comprehensive box office tracking record. Box office results for almost any movie you can think of can be found here.

Common Sense Media: http://www.commonsensemedia.org

Common Sense Media is a non-partisan, not-for-profit organization that recognizes the important part media plays in the lives of children and families and strives to present unbiased information for parents and educators on films, television shows, games, books, Web sites, and music that may not be available elsewhere. This site's rating system is on a sliding scale from age 2 to 17+.

First Showing: http://www.firstshowing.net

First Showing is a great site that offers theater release dates for first run films. Useful background information on pre-production, production, and post-production is also available.

Video ETA: When Entertainment Happens: http://videoeta.com

Video ETA is an essential site for finding DVD release dates.

Teenreads.com http://www.teenreads.com

This site boasts an excellent "Books Into Movies" resource.

CRITICAL BOOKS ON FILMS

Bernstein, Jonathan. *Pretty in Pink: The Golden Age of Teenage Movies*. 1st ed. New York, St. Martin's Griffin, 1997. 230p. $14.95. 9780312151942pa.

Brenner, Robin E. *Understanding Manga and Anime*. Westport, CT, Libraries Unlimited, 2007. 333p. $40.00. 9781591583325pa.

Clements, Jonathan and Helen McCarthy. *The Anime Encyclopedia: A Guide to Japanese Animation Since 1927*. Rev. ed. Berkeley, CA, Stone Bridge Press, 2006. 867p. $29.95. 9781933330105pa.

Ebert, Roger. *Roger Ebert's Four Star Reviews, 1967–2007*. Kansas City, MO, Andrews McMeel, 2007. 944p. $24.99. 9780740771798pa.

Kaveney, Roz. *Teen Dreams: Reading Teen Film and Television from Heathers to Veronica Mars*. 1st ed. New York, I. B. Tauris, 2006. 191p. $14.95. 9781845111847pa.

Kay, Glenn and Michael Rose. *Disaster Movies: A Loud, Long, Explosive, Star Studded Guide to Avalanches, Earthquakes, Floods, Meteors, Sinking Ships, Twisters, Viruses, Killer Bees, Nuclear Fallout, and Alien Attacks in the Cinema!!!* Chicago, Chicago Review Press, 2006. 402p. $18.95. 9781556526121.

Napier, Susan. *Anime from Akira to Howl's Moving Castle: Experiencing Contemporary Japanese Animation*. Rev. ed. New York, Palgrave MacMillan, 2005. 355p. $17.95. 9781403970521pa.

Sarvady, Andrea. *The Ultimate Girls' Movie Survival Guide: What to Rent, Who to Watch, How to Deal*. New York, Simon Spotlight Entertainment, 2004. 255p. $14.95. 0689873735pa.

Turan, Kenneth. *Never Coming to a Theater Near You: A Celebration of a Certain Kind of Movie*. New York, Public Affairs, 2004. 401p. $25.00; $14.00. 9781586482319pa.

Wilson, John. *The Official Razzie Guide: Enjoying the Best of Hollywood's Worst*. New York, Warner Books, 2005. 380p. $14.95. 9780446693340pa.

MAGAZINES AND EZINES

Documentary.org: The International Documentary Association (IDA): http://www.documentary.org

Both magazine and Web site promote and support nonfiction filmmakers around the world.

ICv2: Inside Pop Culture: http://www.ICv2.com

A Web site and magazine, the anime section is required reading for anime selectors.

Moving Pictures Magazine: The Stories Behind the Movies: http://www.movingpicturesmagazine.com

A Web site and magazine, this source analyzes and comments on films in many unique ways and is great reading for the film aficionado.

Student Filmmakers.com: The #1 Educational Resource For Film & Video Makers: http://www.studentfilmmakers.com/

> A Web site and magazine, this source is highly recommended for all libraries with teen patrons that are interested in making their own films.

Video Librarian Online: The Video Review Magazine for Libraries: http://www.videolibrarian.com

> A Web site and magazine, Video Librarian carries current video reviews and excellent articles on new formats and technologies that are aimed at library video selectors. An excellent and highly recommended resource.

WEB SITES FOR TEEN FILMMAKERS

AMDOC: American Documentary: http://www.amdoc.org

> This is the organization responsible for the P.O.V. (Point of View) videos that have been airing on the Public Broadcasting Service since 1988. For over 20 years, P.O.V. (http://www.pbs.org/pov) has broadcast documentary films on PBS. This site has a lot to offer on documentary films.

ACV: Asian CineVision: http://www.asiancinevision.org

> Begun in New York's Chinatown in 1976, this organization supports Asian American filmmakers and media artists and preserves historical information on Asian American videos.

BBC Blast: Film: http://www.bbc.co.uk/blast/film

> From the British Broadcasting Corporation, this is a great site for teen filmmakers.

Center for Asian American Media (CAAM): http://www.asianamericanmedia.org

> Founded in 1980, supported by the Corporation for Public Broadcasting, and a member of the National Minority Consortia, this organization promotes media creations by or of interest to Asian Americans.

The Center for Independent Documentary: http://documentaries.wordpress.com

> Founded in 1981, this very useful nonprofit site offers advice, assistance, and support for independent filmmakers.

Documentary Filmmakers.net: http://www.documentaryfilms.net

> Everything a documentary film viewer, reviewer, or filmmaker might want to know is on this site, including reviews, news, a film directory, and networking opportunities.

Educational Video Center: http://www.evc.org

> This is a non profit organization for young documentary filmmakers.

First Light Movies: http://www.firstlightmovies.com

> Sponsored by the United Kingdom Film Council, this site provides a venue for young filmmakers.

Global Action Project: Youth Making Media: http://www.global-action.org

> This initiative was founded in 1991 to bring information, filmmaking skills, and a forum to youth around the world.

The Independent: The Association of Independent Video and Filmmakers (AIVF): http://www.aivf.org

This webpage's aim is to archive the information of *The Independent Film & Video Monthly* magazine going back to 1978 and to provide historical data along with current information useful for today's filmmakers.

IW indieWIRE: The Leading Source On Independent Films Since 1996: http://www.indiewire.com

News, rumors, and much more on independent films.

Latino Public Broadcasting: http://www.lpbp.org

Created in 1998 by Edward James Olmos and Marlene Dermer, supported by The Corporation for Public Broadcasting, and a member of the National Minority Consortia, this organization promotes media creations by or of interest to Latinos.

NBPC: National Black Programming Consortium: http://www.nbpc.tv

Founded in 1979, supported by the Corporation for Public Broadcasting, and a member of the National Minority Consortia, this organization promotes media creations on television by or of interest to African Americans.

Native American Public Telecommunications (NAPT): http://www.nativetele com.org

Supported by the Corporation for Public Broadcasting and a member of the National Minority Consortia, this organization promotes media creations by or of interest to Native Americans. VisionMaker Video is a service of NAPT that supports the creation of Native American media and is a great source for Native American videos.

Pacific Islanders in Communication: http://www.piccom.org

Founded in 1991 in Hawaii, supported by the Corporation for Public Broadcasting, and a member of the National Minority Consortia, this organization promotes cultural awareness by or of interest to the Pacific Island community.

Reel Grrls: http://www.reelgrrls.org

Started in 2001, this program's aim is to address the inequity of the small numbers of women in the filmmaking profession by giving a venue and dispersing information to young female filmmakers.

Youth Views: http://www.pbs.org/pov/utils/youthviews.html

Begun in 2000 and a part of Public Broadcasting System's Point of View series, this is a peer-led initiative to encourage and support media efforts created by young people. The Youth Views library contains downloadable videos made by young people under the age of 21.

BOOKS ON FILMMAKING FOR TEENS

Ang, Tom. *Digital Video: An Introduction.* New York, DK Publishing, 2006. 224p. $15.00. 9780756616007pa.

Ascher, Steven and Edward Pincus. *The Filmmaker's Handbook: a Comprehensive Guide for the Digital Age.* 3rd ed. New York, Plume, 2008. 8322p. $25.00. 9780452286788pa.

Boorstin, Jon. *Making Movies Work: Thinking Like a Filmmaker.* 2nd rev. ed. Los Angeles, CA, Silman-James Press, 1995. 224p. $19.95. 9781879505278pa.

Corey, Melinda. *The American Film Institute Desk Reference.* 1st American ed. New York, N.Y., DK Publishing, 2002. 608p. $40.00. 0789489341pa.

Cristiano, Giuseppe. *Storyboard Design Course: Principles, Practice, and Techniques.* (Hauppauge, NY: Barron's Educational Series). 2007. 192p. $24.99. 9780764137327pa.

Figgis, Mike. *Digital Filmmaking.* 1st ed. New York, Faber and Faber, 2007. 158p. $13.95. 9780571226252pa.

Hamlett, Christina. *Could It Be a Movie?: How to Get Your Ideas From Out of Your Head and Up On The Screen.* Studio City, CA, M. Wiese Productions, 2005. 269p. $18.95. 9780941188949pa.

Hamlett, Christina. *Screen Teen Writers: How Young Screenwriters Can Find Success.* 1st ed. Colorado Springs: Meriwether Publishing, 2002. 248p. $16.95. 9781566080789pa.

Hamlett, Christina. *Screenwriting for Teens: The 100 Principles of Screenwriting Every Budding Writer Must Know.* Studio City, CA, M. Wiese Productions, 2006. 228p. $18.95. 9781932907186pa.

Hancock, Hugh and Johnnie Ingram. *Machinima For Dummies.* Hoboken, NJ, Wiley, 2007. 403p. $29.99. 9780470096918pa.

Heimberg, Justin. *The Official Movie Plot Generator: 27,000 Hilarious Movie Plot Combinations.* Los Angeles, CA, Brothers Heimberg Publishing, 2004. Unpaged. $15.95. 0974043915.

Lanier, Tony and Clay Nichols. *Filmmaking for Teens: Pulling Off Your Shorts.* Studio City, CA, M. Wiese Productions, 2005. 179p. $18.95. 1932907041pa.

Lawrence, Colton. *Big Fat Paycheck: A Young Person's Guide to Writing for the Movies.* New York, Bantam Books for Young Readers, 2004. 269p. $11.99. 9780553131222.

Patmore, Chris. *Moviemaking Course: Principles, Practice, and Techniques: The Ultimate Guide for the Aspiring Filmmaker.* Hauppuage, NY, Barron's Educational Series, 2005. 144p. $19.99. 9780764131915pa.

Pogue, David. *iMovie '08 & iDVD: The Missing Manual.* Sebastopol, CA, O'Reilly Media, 2008. 448p. $39.99. 9780596516192pa.

Press, Skip. *The Complete Idiot's Guide to Screenwriting.* 2nd ed. Indianapolis, IN, Alpha, 2004. 390p. $18.95. 9781592572251pa.

Schellhardt, Laura. *Screenwriting for Dummies.* 1st ed. New York, Wiley Publishing, 2004. 335p. $19.99. 0764554867pa.

Schwartz, Mark Evan. *How to Write: A Screenplay.* New York, Continuum, 2005. 110p. $14.95. 9780826428172pa.

Shaner, Pete and Gerald Everett Jones, *Digital Filmmaking for Teens.* Boston, MA, Thomson Course Technology PTR, 2005. 256p. $24.99. 9781592006038pa.

Shulman, Mark and Hazlett Krog. *Attack of the Killer Video Book: Tips and Tricks for Young Directors.* Toronto, ON, New York, Annick Press, 2004. 64p. $12.95. 1550378406pa.

Stieff, Josef. *The Complete Idiot's Guide to Independent Filmmaking.* 1st ed. New York, Alpha, 2005. 363p. $18.95. 1592573908pa.
Stoller, Bryan Michael and Jerry Lewis. *Filmmaking For Dummies.* 1st ed. Hoboken, NJ, Wiley Publishing, 2003. 354p. $19.99. 0764524763pa.

ARTICLES

Conlon, Susan. "Putting Your Teens in Focus With Films." *VOYA*, August 2007. pp. 212–215.
Halsall, Jane. "The Anime Revelation: How I learned to love Japanese animation and changed our teen video collection forever," *SLJ'S Guide to Graphic Novels*, Supplement to *School Library Journal*, August 2004.
"Documentary Filmmaking for Teens," Understanding Media: Media Literacy on the Web. Understanding Media Staff. http://www.understandingmedia. caom/art030.htm.

AFTERWORD

A good friend of ours tells a story about driving across the Bonneville Salt Flats: you drive and you drive and you drive, but the mountains in front of you never seem to get any closer. Writing a book is like that: you write and you write and you write, but the end never seems to be any nearer. The trick, we are told, is to look into the rearview mirror and see how far the book has come. So it's time to do just that.

As this book has already suggested, a good film collection is a critical part of serving teen patrons and deserves any and all time and money that your library can devote to it. In addition, there are distinct differences in selecting for teens as opposed to children or adults. Resources for serving teens aren't as readily available, for example, and locating information on what's new and hot can be both difficult and daunting. Despite this extra effort needed to build a teen collection, the endeavor can be especially rewarding.

Remember that teens themselves are your best resource, so talk to them often and make sure that you listen. Teens aren't as forthcoming or as trusting as children, and they are generally not as articulate as adults. However, once you've established yourself as someone who listens to their likes and dislikes, you may be surprised by the amount of useful input they give you towards building your collection.

Listening to teens offers you a continuing education program on what's new in popular culture and in technology. What you can learn will change day by day, but much of what you learn, especially about new gadgets, will put you well ahead of everyone else. Librarians who work with teens are at the cutting edge of popular culture and information/entertainment technology.

Work hard to make sure that teens don't become alienated from libraries and librarians. Given all your responsibilities and despite all your best intentions, you may lose track of your teen patrons even now. However, if you don't stay on the ball, you risk losing teens as patrons, as future voters and taxpayers, and as future librarians. The danger isn't just the age old one of teens drifting away from libraries when their information and entertainment needs are not met. The new problem is that teens have access to other sources of information and entertainment that could make libraries irrelevant for them.

Patrons become library users when the library fulfills a need. They develop a special relationship with libraries when their informational and recreational needs are exceeded, and that usually requires a librarian. When you listen, ask questions, and don't pass judgments on your teen patrons, whether you know it or not, you are making a difference. You won't know what that difference is since a teen isn't likely to tell you, but let's hope it is a positive one.

One great pleasure of working with teens is being the first person to suggest they watch what may become their favorite movie of all time. You get to spread the word about Monty Python, the Marx Brothers, *Casablanca*, and *Caddy Shack*. Another equally great pleasure is being told by a teen about *your* next favorite movie, one that might be a classic for the ages, and that wasn't reviewed by the professional or popular press. Remember, when you talk to a teen, you might just learn something yourself.

INDEX

About the Authors

JANE HALSALL graduated summa cum laude from the University of Illinois at Urbana/Champaign Graduate School of Library and Information Science, where she was in the first class of the LEEP distance-learning program. She became been head of young peoples' services at McHenry Public Library in 1997. She has spoken at the American Association of School Librarians National Conference in Kansas City (2003) and done solo presentations for the Illinois Library Association in 2004 and 2006. In 1998, she was awarded the Multi-Type Librarian of the Year Award from the North Suburban Library System of Illinois. She has been an anime reviewer for *Video Librarian* and is currently an audio/visual reviewer for *School Library Journal*, which has published over 100 of her book and film reviews. She is serving on the Young Adult Librarian Service Association's Fabulous Films for Young Adults Committee for the 2008–2010 term. Her interest in serving teens began when coping with two gifted teenagers of her own.

R. WILLIAM EDMINSTER, a graduate of Lawrence University and of Rosary College [now Dominican University] Graduate School of Library and Information Science, has been assistant director at McHenry Public Library since 1993 and was acting director during 2007. Although his background is in technical services, colleagues have repeatedly reminded him that he is qualified to speak and write about service to teens because he still remembers what it was like to be a teen.

The authors first began speaking publicly in 1998 about the importance of including popular materials in library collections as a means of attracting teens. They have given presentations together at Public Library Associations conferences (2004, 2006), at the Illinois Library Association conference (2002), at The National Council of Teachers of English's Assembly on Literature for Adolescents (2000), at the AnimeCentral Annual Conference (2006), and for various library systems in Illinois and Wisconsin over the years. They were the keynote speakers at Mayor Daley's Book Club Facilitators' Orientation for the 2002–2003 school year. In addition, they served as consultants for the Lake County [Illinois] Discovery Museum's exhibition on anime, named "Anime-zing: The World of Japanese Animation," which ran during 2005 and 2006.